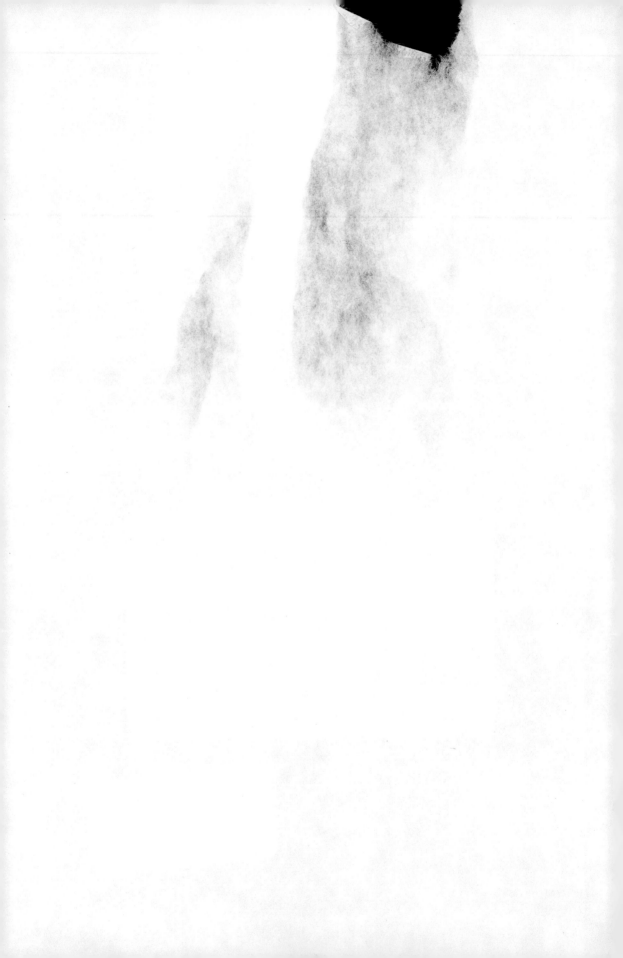

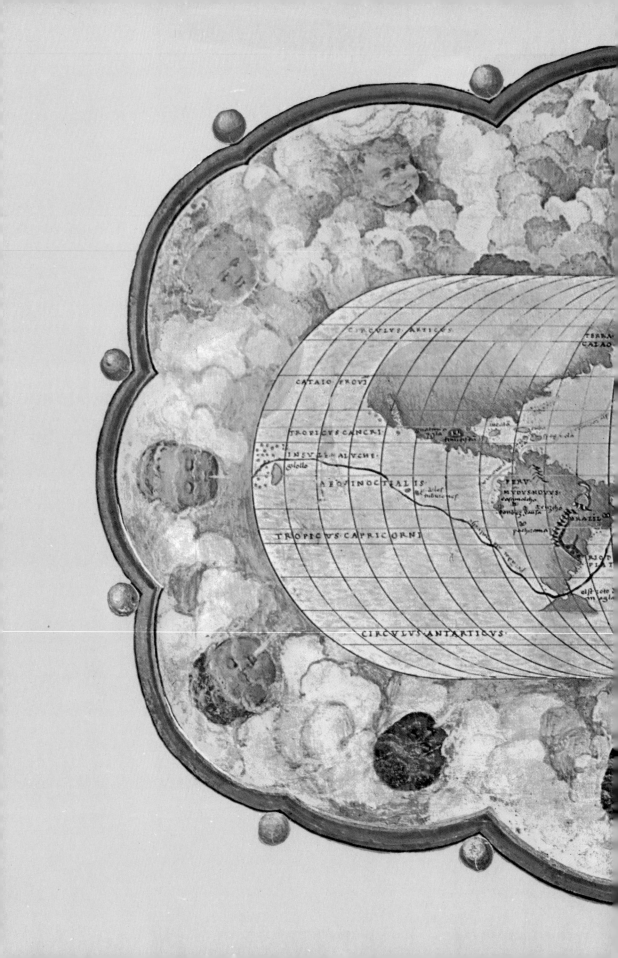

AMERICAN HERITAGE
ILLUSTRATED HISTORY
OF THE UNITED STATES

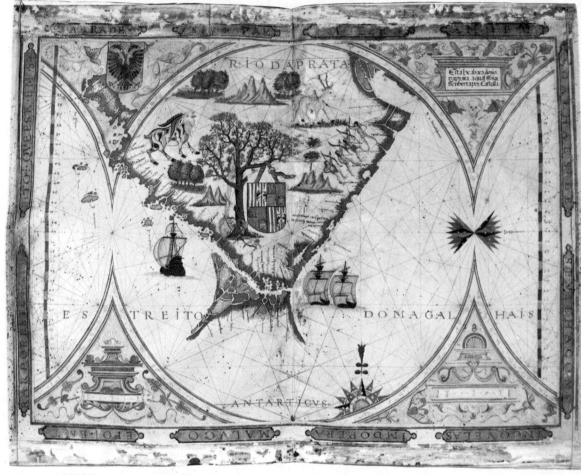

A 1568 Portuguese map by Vaz Dourado of the southern tip of South America.

FRONT COVER: *Detail from The Debarkation of Christopher Columbus.*
U.S. NAVAL ACADEMY MUSEUM

FRONT ENDSHEET: *Magellan's world voyage traced from a map made around 1545.*
JOHN CARTER BROWN LIBRARY

BACK ENDSHEET: *Sir Francis Drake's fleet in harbor at Santo Domingo, 1585.*
NEW YORK PUBLIC LIBRARY

BACK COVER: *An Engraving (top left) of John Smith, from his book about his 1614 New England voyage; a 1600 engraving of an Indian chief, angered by the greed of Spanish conquistadors (top right); Henry Hudson sailed the Half Moon (bottom) up the river that bears his name in 1609, as Indians watched from the shore.*
LIBRARY OF CONGRESS; NEW YORK PUBLIC LIBRARY; LIBRARY OF CONGRESS

25947

AMERICAN HERITAGE ILLUSTRATED HISTORY OF THE UNITED STATES

VOLUME 1

THE NEW WORLD

LIBRARY EDITION
with Index in Volume 19

SILVER BURDETT PRESS, INC.

1989

© 1989, 1988, 1971, 1967, 1963 by American Heritage, a division of Forbes Inc. All rights reserved. No part of this work
may be reproduced or transmitted in any form or by any means, electronic or mechanical, including photocopying and
recording, or by any information storage or retrieval system without permission in writing from the publisher.

Library of Congress Catalog Card Number: 89-50419
ISBN 0-382-09858-7 (Vol. 1)
ISBN 0-382-09878-1 (Set)

This 1989 revised edition is published and distributed by Silver Burdett Press, Inc., Prentice Hall Building, Englewood Cliffs, NJ 07632
by arrangement with American Heritage, a division of Forbes, Inc.

Manufactured in the United States of America

AMERICAN HERITAGE ILLUSTRATED HISTORY OF THE UNITED STATES

VOLUME 1

THE NEW WORLD

BY ROBERT G. ATHEARN

Created in Association with the
Editors of AMERICAN HERITAGE

and for the updated edition
MEDIA PROJECTS INCORPORATED

CHOICE PUBLISHING, INC.

New York

AMERICAN HERITAGE
ILLUSTRATED HISTORY OF THE UNITED STATES

CREATED AND DESIGNED BY THE EDITORS OF
AMERICAN HERITAGE STAFF FOR THE ORIGINAL EDITION

Richard M. Ketchum, *Senior Editor*
Murray Belsky, *Editorial Art Director*
Murray Belsky, *Editorial Director*
Kenneth W. Leish, *Vice-President and General Manager Books*

STAFF FOR THE UPDATED EDITION
Created in Association with MEDIA PROJECTS INCORPORATED

Carter Smith, *Executive Editor*
Sherwood Harris, *Editor*
Bernard Schleifer, *Art Director/Design Consultant*
Tom Carey, Jill Roberts, *Chief Researchers*
Geoffrey C. Ward, *Principal Editorial Consultant*

AMERICAN HERITAGE, A DIVISION OF FORBES INC.

Timothy C. Forbes, *President*
Scott E. Masterson, *General Manager*
Barbara M. Strauch, *Director, Book Division*

CHOICE PUBLISHING, INC.

The Encyclopedic Section found at the end of each volume contains individual entries, arranged alphabetically, on the persons, places, and events mentioned in the main text, as well as other important figures and events in the period of American history covered in that volume. A cross-reference within an encyclopedic entry indicates that a separate entry appears elsewhere in that section. Certain prominent persons and significant events, however, may be mentioned within the entries of one Encyclopedic Section but appear as individual entries in another volume. To locate the main entry, consult the Index in Volume 18.

Library of Congress Catalog Card Number: 87-73399
ISBN 0-945260-01-6
ISBN 0-945260-00-8

This 1988 edition is published anad distributed by Choice Publishing, Inc., 53 Watermill Lane, Great Neck, NY 11021 by arrangement with American Heritage, a division of Forbes, Inc.

Manufactured in the United States of America
10 9 8 7 6 5 4 3

CONTENTS OF THE COMPLETE SERIES

Editor's Note to the Revised Edition
Introduction by ALLAN NEVINS
Main text by ROBERT G. ATHEARN

EACH VOLUME CONTAINS AN ENCYCLOPEDIC SECTION; MASTER INDEX IN VOLUME 18

Editor's Note to the Updated Edition

When President John F. Kennedy wrote the foreword to the first edition of the *American Heritage Illustrated History of the United States* in 1963, he quoted the writer, John Dos Passos: "A knowledge of history is a means of strength—'When there is a quicksand of fear under men's reasoning, a sense of continuity with generations gone before can stretch like a lifeline across the scary present.' "

The ancient Chinese saying that "It is a curse to be born in interesting times" has never seemed more apt than for our recent history. President Kennedy, like each American president since World War II, faced incredible challenges in an increasingly complex world. Each has enjoyed triumphs and suffered defeats. Much has gone on.

The original edition of *The American Heritage Illustrated History of the United States* was purchased by hundreds of thousands of families. Critics and teachers praised the book's low price—made possible by mass marketing—and its accessible, richly illustrated treatment of history.

Inspired by celebrations of the bicentennial of the founding of the republic and the signing of the Constitution, American Heritage and Choice Publishing have updated the original sixteen volumes in the series and added two entirely new volumes dealing with our most recent history.

As in earlier editions, each volume contains several narrative chapters, describing in clear objective terms what occurred in the spheres of foreign and domestic affairs in each period. The arts, science, and entertainment of the time are featured in full color in "Special Picture Portfolios" and a "Close-Up on History"—an illustrated essay by a noted historian—gives an in-depth assessment of a key leader, event, or issue. Finally, each volume contains an illustrated Encyclopedic Section, with concise individual entries—arranged alphabetically— covering the lives and contributions of the leading personalities of the era and the most important issues of the times. (This feature has been particularly well received by students who use the series for research.) Volume Eighteen contains a Comprehensive Index.

One of the most challenging matters for the editors of an illustrated popular history is the selection of images that best capture the momentous—or even mundane, but representative— events that are our history.

Because newspapers, magazines, and particularly television, bombard us with images some become clichés. Should one use again the heart-rending image of a young boy at the state funeral of his father, an assassinated president, a police chief executing a Viet Cong suspect in a Saigon street, or the wonderful pictures of Americans on the moon—or on the great wall of China?

The answer, of course, is that while these are familiar to many of us of a certain age, they may not be to younger readers. And, if an image of skyrockets exploding over the Statue of Liberty is a cliché, it is also a classic.

As chronicled in these pages, the nine post-World War II presidents often differed on matters of politics and doctrine but, as the following feature makes evident, they all loved and respected our history. We know readers of the updated edition of *The American Heritage Illustrated History of the United States* share that feeling.

CARTER SMITH
Executive Editor for the Updated Series

NETHERLANDS

SPAIN

ENGLAND

PORTUGAL

FRANCE

CONTENTS OF VOLUME 1

Harry S Truman Dwight D. Eisenhower John F. Kennedy Lyndon B. Johnson

Why History?

Harry S Truman

"There is nothing new in the world except the history you do not know."

Dwight D. Eisenhower

". . . The only sensible approach is to inform yourselves thoroughly before drawing conclusions. I suggest not only that you read the newspapers and periodicals but that you also study deeply the history of our country and of all humankind. I particularly recommend to you the basic documents of our American civilization, the Declaration of Independence and the Constitution of the United States. Read them and ponder their meaning. They are my handbooks. I keep them on a shelf right behind my desk, and a week rarely passes that I do not refer to them for help in clarifying my own thinking . . ."

John F. Kennedy

"A knowledge of history is . . . a means of strength. When Americans fight for individual liberty, they have Thomas Jefferson and James Madison behind them; when they strive for social justice, they strive alongside Andrew Jackson and Franklin Roosevelt; when they work for peace and a world community, they work with Woodrow Wilson; when they fight and die in wars to make men free, they fight and die with Abraham Lincoln. Historic continuity with the past, as Justice Oliver Wendell Holmes said, 'Is not a duty; it is only a necessity.' "

Lyndon B. Johnson

". . . We believe that history, when it is written, will not be the story of the doubters. Their fate, in the future, will not be in the headlines, but it will just be a footnote here and there. For we know that history deals with acts, with dreams that have been translated into reality, with victories that are won or lost. History deals with promises made and promises kept."

Richard M. Nixon

"As we read the pages of history, we find those pages strewn with the wreckage of great civilizations in the past who lost their leadership just at the time that they were the richest, and at the time when they had the capability of being the strongest. They lost their leadership because their leader class failed to meet the responsibilities and the challenges of the times. They, in other words, turned away from greatness. They grew soft. They did not welcome the opportunity to continue to lead, which was their destiny at that time, and those civilizations are forgotten except as they are read about in the pages of history."

Richard M. Nixon *Gerald R. Ford*   *James Earl Carter*   *Ronald Reagan*

Gerald R. Ford

''An indispensable element of the strength, the freedom, and the constructive world leadership of this nation is the knowledge and appreciation of our history, of who we are, where we are, and how we arrived here . . . working together we can build an America that does not merely celebrate history, but writes it; that offers limited government and unlimited opportunity; that concerns itself with the quality of life; that proves individual liberty is the key to mutual achievement and national progress.''

James Earl Carter

''While president, I sought to make my administration the most open in history. Secrecy is necessary at times, but this should not be assumed to protect officials from public scrutiny. I maintain my conviction that in our government of the people, for the people, and by the people, the people have the right to know and the need to know what their government is about.''

Ronald Reagan

''For a democracy to function, its people must understand not only reading, writing, and arithmetic but literature, history, and values. Someone once said that 'if you think education is expensive, you should try ignorance.' And that sums up the situation pretty well. To be American means to understand that education is the key that opens up the golden door of opportunity . . . No civilization can survive and grow if it does not learn the lessons of its own history.''

George Bush

"Our American heritage is grounded in a living Constitution. Because the document lives, it has enhanced our freedoms and supported a system that seeks to unleash the God-given talents of every individual to grow and prosper. The energy that gives our Constitution life and meaning comes from the American people. Not until we look at the range of history and the experiences of other nations can we fully appreciate the miracle of 1787. The responsibility for preserving, protecting, and refining our living Constitution is shared by all of us. Our system is sound. Imperfections remain 1787–1987, we the people continue on."

George Bush

INTRODUCTION

ALLEN NEVINS

How are we to approach our American history? It is, first of all, a throbbing, human, and vital story—dramatic and colorful. Any author who makes it fascinating, without falsifying it, is probably telling it well.

Every generation has to rewrite its history. But each new version has to have a pattern, a design, and within limits each of us has a right to say what it should be.

The most usual pattern has been to make our past a grand success story. That was the approach that George Bancroft used a century ago and which others have followed. The voice of our best American commentators has nearly always been an optimistic voice, and foreign observers have struck the same note of optimism. All describe achievement after achievement—the raw continent settled, independence gained, an efficient government established, the scope of democracy widened, national unity confirmed in the Civil War, slavery abolished, poverty increasingly reduced, opportunity thrown open to all, two perilous world wars won, and the leadership of free peoples gallantly assumed.

This approach to American history seems the more convincing because our record over the past two centuries does contrast happily with that of less fortunate lands. But if we look carefully at the seamy side of the record and weigh the irrational, blundering, wasteful, and corrupt conduct of large groups and their leaders, we may well have doubts. The tendency of Americans simply to drift when strenuous and well-planned action was needed has often been especially distressing. Ours is a success story, but it is not that alone.

Another approach to our past has it as the story of an expanding democracy. Much can be said for this concept, which brings the plain people into the center of the picture. It has the seal of the high authority. The distinctive trait of our republic, said Abraham Lincoln, is that it was "conceived in liberty and dedicated to the proposition that all men are created equal"—that is, it was by the principles of its origin democratic. Europeans have always regarded the United States as the world's major experiment in democracy.

But democracy is an ideal at once simple and complex. It has to be broken down into three distinct parts: *Political Democracy,* which we have gained and kept only by constant fighting; *social democracy,* of which we have had more than most nations, but which has not prevented the emergence in every generation of class lines; and *economic democracy,* of which we have had little for long periods.

History shows that these three parts of democracy are often in partial conflict. For example, our lack of economic democracy between 1870 and 1910, when colossal fortunes stood beside abysmal poverty, gravely crippled our political and social democracy.

IF BOTH THE success-story and the expanding democracy analysis of our history are inadequate and often misleading, what then? James Truslow Adams declared that the true key to an understanding of our past is to be found in the search for the "American dream." The Europeans who came in successive waves believed that they could hew out a better destiny, that they could find more security, more freedom, more scope for their talents, more happiness—in short, a richer, nobler life. Sometimes the American dream failed, as in the terrible tragedy of the Civil War and its aftermath; never has it been perfectly realized. Moreover, it has varied from section to section—the Southern planter's dream of 1850 was totally different from that of the Northern farmer; from group to group—the dream of the frontiersman was quite unlike that of the immigrant in the New York sweatshop; from era to era—an industrial nation with a population approaching 250,000,000 can make but limited use of the Jeffersonian dream, so well adapted to a youthful agrarian republic. Yet the American dream remains a guiding light for interpreting our history.

What we have in common is a *national character*. So we believe, and so the whole world believes. It changes from generation to generation, from century to century. Assuredly it is less individualistic than it was in the days of the founding fathers, but it is more disciplined, more social-minded and world-conscious. Can anyone doubt that our faith in ourselves and our destiny is any less fervent? There is evidence that it has even deepened. We are far wealthier now; we have witnessed an explosion in population, of affluence, of leisure. But has not our idealism kept pace with our material advance?

When Sir Ernest Baker wrote his *National Character and the Factors in Its Formation* a generation ago, he divided the formative factors into two groups—material and spiritual. He listed the chief material factors as racial (genetic), geographical, and economic. He gave them only a third of his book. The spiritual factors are much more numerous. They include law, governmental institutions, religion, language, literature, thought and education. To *them* he gave fully two-thirds, indicating that he believed the greatest forces in history to have been the spiritual ones. What single element, he asks at one point, stands above all others in shaping English civilization? His answer is the Common Law of England—the only great system of jurisprudence in the world besides the Roman. Barker believes it has had a deeper influence on the temper and behavior of the British people than any other single force.

READERS OF THIS work may be repaid in many ways for the time and attention they give to it, for it objectively presents the basic facts of American history, with enough interpretation to stimulate further pondering over means and ends, causes and effects.

All in all, readers will find here a story varied in human interest, dramatic impact, and at times inspiring—illustrated by drawings, paintings, and photographs, many by eyewitnesses or contemporaries, of a variety and quality never before offered in such a work. Readers will also find food for imagination—events and achievements that can stir the mind as few novelists can ever stir it, because what *happened* far transcends any make-believe.

Allen Nevins, 1890–1971, has been called "the foremost American historian of his generation." He was a teacher of history at Columbia University for more than 30 years, and the author of more than 30 major works on all periods of American history.

CHAPTER 1

EUROPE MOVES WEST

Before dawn on October 12, 1492, three small vessels under the command of a Genoese sailor named Christopher Columbus pushed their way westward near a tiny island in the Bahamas. Suddenly Rodrigo de Triana, a lookout on the *Pinta,* sighted a shadowy form dead ahead. It was too massive to be a floating object. With the cry *"Tierra! Tierra!"* he brought the ship awake, and quickly its captain signaled Columbus of the discovery. "You *did* find land!" Columbus shouted to him. "I give you 5,000 maravedis as a bonus." With sails shortened, the *Santa María, Pinta,* and *Niña* hove to, their crews waiting impatiently for sunrise.

Daylight brought a view of the first land seen in the Western Hemisphere by any Europeans, save perhaps the earlier Norsemen. On the western side of the island the seamen found a protected bay and, as the startled natives ashore looked on, a small boat bearing the royal standard of Spain was landed. After kneeling on the sand

Columbus plants the Cross in the New World, thus opens the great period of exploration of the Americas. From a 1665 fresco.

and thanking God for a safe voyage, Columbus arose and named the bit of land San Salvador. Relations were then begun with the natives, whom the newcomers called Indians. Red caps, glass beads, and other articles of small value were bartered for skeins of cotton thread, parrots, and darts. European contact with the American native would continue for nearly 400 years, until he was traded out of almost all his land and belongings.

After a day or so of rest, the explorer took his ships deeper into the Caribbean, sighting Cuba, which he explained to his men was Japan. In December they discovered Hispaniola and there put up a small fort, garrisoning it with a handful of men. By March of 1493, Columbus landed at Lisbon and announced to the world that he had seen the Indies. The Portuguese were both excited and dubious. Here was a man who had accomplished by sailing westward what they had taken a century to do by rounding the Cape of Good Hope.

What caused Columbus to make a journey of such length and danger? Did it mean that Europe was overcrowded, fully exploited economically, shorn of all its opportunities? Or was this simply a breed of man endowed with an overdeveloped sense of adventure? The answer perhaps lies in Spain's eagerness to keep abreast of the Portuguese, now Europe's most renowned navigators, and to participate in the greatest expansion the Christian world had yet experienced.

During Columbus' century—the 15th—Europe began to emerge from its old local isolations. The feudal system, tied to the local authority of minor warlords, was beginning to give way to the modern national state, a more powerful and permanent political organization. As the authority of the feudal lords dwindled, many of those who had lived under them moved toward the cities. Europe, still predominantly agricultural, was now going in a direction that took men away from a mere subsistence economy, where they raised most of their necessities on a small plot of ground, to a money, or profit, economy. As the artisan class began to grow, and articles for sale were produced in larger quantities, the enterprising merchant (the traveling salesman of his time) began to move out in an ever-widening circle from his home town. Local trade routes, little used for hundreds of years, now saw a growing traffic, and peddlers passing through told fascinating tales of other areas. This resulted in a curiosity to know more about lands farther away. The increased travel and trade meant that the methods of transpor-

Marco Polo is seen setting out fr
24 years later, and his report of t

enice in 1271 on his journey to China. He returned
ch new world in the East intrigued the Europeans.

tation, particularly by water, were soon to be expanded and improved. It also meant the rise of the city.

The rise of the city was extremely important to later explorations. Although by 1500 only one-tenth of Europe's population was urban, the growing towns were strategically located from the standpoint of commerce. London, Hamburg, Antwerp, and Lisbon were built near the mouths of rivers, while Paris, Mainz, and Ghent stood close to river junctions. By today's standards these places were small. When Columbus sailed for America, London had only 50,000 people. Constantinople, Europe's largest city, had 250,000; Paris, 200,000; Ghent, 135,000. But they were populous and important for their time, and the association with water transportation destined them to be the metropolitan areas of the future. It can be questioned whether, without such places, we would have had universities, great inventions, or a flourishing art—or, for that matter, whether Columbus would have made his great find. As centers of trade, Europe's cities now became not only powerful independent bastions, but springboards for further economic venture.

If Europe at this time was broken into small political segments, it still had a religious unity. The Catholic Church was dominant and all-powerful. Yet the Church served as a stimulant rather than a deterrent to most businesses and to commerce. For example, its crusading fervor took men to all parts of the known world in search of converts, and as they moved around, they could not help noticing new and different articles that would be useful in trade. Even the monastic orders were producers of such salable goods as wine, grain, and cloth. Finally, extensive travel back and forth from all Europe to the Continent's religious capital, Rome, served to broaden men's knowledge of opportunities throughout the land.

The Crusades, which during the 12th and 13th centuries attempted to free the Holy Land from non-Christians, stirred Europe considerably. In some cases the great movement amounted to a nationwide effort as kings were persuaded to employ large forces in the Middle East. The overall result was that thousands of individuals, from baronial knights down to propertyless workers, traveled farther away from home than they ever had before. Eastward, beyond the Mediterranean, they encountered a strange new civilization, rich beyond belief. Spices, silks, and other luxury items excited their imaginations, and if they could not all bring home samples of

The merchants in this 1497 miniature were part of the Hanseatic League, a mercantile association of German towns. Business is discussed in the city of Hamburg, while the ships lying in the harbor prepare to carry metalware, silks, and linens from the cities of northern Europe to the seaports of the eastern Baltic.

14

Godfrey of Bouillon, leader of the first crusading army, prepares to sail to the East, as confident as William the Conqueror. In fact, his ship looked more like one of William's than does this fanciful, overcrowded 14th-century vessel.

their finds, they certainly carried back stories of all they had seen.

Transportation facilities developed rapidly, as always, when wars are fought at a distance. More soldiers had to be moved farther than ever before, and out of the need arose an important shipbuilding industry at such places of embarkation as the Italian cities. No sea captain likes to come home with an empty vessel, and be-

fore the religious wars were very old, large quantities of Eastern goods made their appearance in Europe. Livestock in Europe was small and rangy, all muscle and bone, and its meat was much more palatable after an application of such spices as pepper. Here was a type of merchandise that the seamen could bring back in quantity and sell at a high price. Then there were the nobles who were eager to have fine cloth and jewels with which to bedeck themselves and set themselves apart from the lesser nobles or even their own serfs. No enterprising businessmen could overlook this market. Out of the possibilities for sudden gain arose a powerful and active merchant class. These men were ingenious, ambitious, willing to take a risk, and always desirous of finding new sources of goods and new methods of bringing them to market. If they read of Marco Polo's travels, their determination to expand operations doubtless rose to new heights.

The Turks—unwelcome interlopers

But in 1453 a trade barrier appeared. The Turks captured Constantinople, at the crossroads of this new and rich trade route, and with the conquest of Cairo in 1517 they would complete their domination of the Near East. This did not mean the end of trade. It meant only that another middleman had been added to the string that already handed on the goods from faraway lands. The Europeans now would have to deal with the Turks, or find a new route that would cut out these hopeful associates. It was not any refusal on the part of the Turk to join the new gold rush that caused European Christians to seek other routes. By circumventing the interlopers, merchants simply could realize greater dividends from their ventures. If an all-water route to the East could be found, it would mean cheaper transportation, larger

profits, and the pleasant prospect of dealing the Turks out of a new and highly profitable game. The idea was inviting enough to make adventurous people take long chances.

The upsurge in commercial life had a good many ramifications. People were eager to learn more about other parts of the world, and the resulting intellectual activity sparked a renaissance in European cultural life. Their curiosity stemmed from a desire to find additional sources of luxuries, better methods of transportation, and wider markets for distribution. The emphasis was on the material—personal acquisition and gain. In their desire for worldly fame and personal achievement, men turned to the Greek classics to see what secrets they would reveal. When they found suggestions that the world was round and perhaps the East might be reached by sailing westward, they were interested. The idea was appealing because their experimentations had produced more efficient means of navigation, making such a journey feasible. The compass and the astrolabe (an instrument used to determine latitude) now were rather widely used. Charts and maps were constantly being improved and expanded. By 1600, explorers were better equipped than ever to sail great distances from home. With the powerful commercial stimulus, their ventures became more and more bold. The age of discovery was at hand.

Expeditions to discover new trade routes could be organized in several ways. The Italians learned early that the joint-stock company was one method. A

Prince Henry the Navigator

way to fabled India would be clear. His conviction finally paid off. By 1488, Bartholomeu Diaz had rounded the Cape of Good Hope, and 10 years later Vasco da Gama reached India. When asked what had brought them so far, the sailors answered, "Christians and spices." Shortly the new trade route around Africa was in use, and the late Prince Henry's determination to develop it had caused a commercial revolution. Within a few years the Portuguese had plunged eastward all the way to China and Japan. No longer were the Italian cities the focal point in the Eastern trade. The center had shifted from the Mediterranean, now a mere lake, to the Atlantic, and the Iberian Peninsula soared to new importance.

Columbus puts Spain ahead

Because the rival Portuguese were so successful at exploration, the Spanish were willing to listen to the proposals of Columbus. Perhaps in more normal times his theory that the Indies could be reached more simply by sailing due west than by using the long and dangerous route around Africa might have been ignored. But the Spanish, whose rise to national power happened to coincide with the great period of maritime expansion, wanted some of the benefits of the new trade for themselves. After many doubts and delays, King Ferdinand and Queen Isabella gave Columbus the financial support necessary to carry out his geographical investiga-

number of merchants might join in a venture, sharing the risk and the profits. The Crusades had shown that such an organization as the Church, combined with the resources of wealthy knights, could launch extensive projects. But it was the rise of the national state in Europe, whose various monarchs were avid for increased wealth and power, that saw most of the successful explorations completed. Prominent among these new nations was little Portugal, jutting westward into the Atlantic, and most strategically located for an important place in the coming world trade.

Portugal's young Prince Henry, who was to become known to the world as The Navigator, pushed one exploration after another southward along the African coast during the 15th century. He believed that when the huge land mass was passed, the tions. Sailing westward from Spain on August 3, 1492, he pushed his little fleet deep into the unknown Atlantic and raised a landfall by October 12. He was convinced that he had fulfilled his ambition to reach the Indies.

Although it soon developed that Columbus had found something other than the Indies in 1492, the Spanish continued to exploit and enlarge upon his discoveries. Columbus himself made three other voyages within the next few years, and before long Spain had embarked upon a colonial effort in the Americas that was not to end until 1898. Rival European nations were quick to see that the Admiral of the Ocean Sea had found something important, and soon their own ships headed west. As early as 1497 and 1498, John Cabot, flying British colors, ranged along the coast of present Canada and the United States. Giovanni da Verrazano, representing the French in 1524, coasted off the same shores. A generation before, in 1500, a Portuguese navigator named Pedro de Cabral claimed that he had touched a part of South America, and his sponsors soon hoisted their flag on what would be called Brazil. Meanwhile, Spanish ships penetrated western waters in larger numbers, expanding upon the original claims. Vasco de Balboa boldly crossed the Isthmus of Panama in 1513 and found still another ocean! A Florentine merchant named Amerigo Vespucci wrote so glowingly of one of these expeditions that a German geographer suggested

the newly opened part of the world be called America. Since it had been called everything from the Land of the Parrots to New India, to no one's satisfaction, the new and shorter name stuck. Columbus, who died impoverished, could not even will his name to the greatest discovery of the age.

After the initial disappointment at not having found the Indies wore off, the Spanish and all other Europeans realized that something of general interest had been uncovered. The leaders of the old continent, now on the verge of an economic boom, were deeply interested in enlarging their supply of

Giovanni da Verrazano

19

that well-known medium of exchange, gold. The prospect of finding additional products for exchange or manufacture also excited their appetites. The desire for personal wealth and the possibility of sudden financial ascendancy powered the drive of the Spanish in particular to exploit to the limit their new findings, and the Portuguese, fearful of losing out, complained about it. To settle any argument, the Pope drew a line down the map of the Atlantic in 1493, giving to Portugal eastern Brazil, Africa, the East Indies. Spain received most of America.

True, the new land did not yield up large troves of gems, bales of silks, or quantities of Oriental spices, but there were some returns to be had and they were not lost upon the explorers. As early as 1512, on the island of Hispaniola, where Columbus had founded the first colony in the Americas, the Spaniards were extracting a million dollars in gold annually. Aside from the mining, there were agricultural resources. Sugar cane, introduced into the West Indies by Columbus, promised to yield a profitable return. Equally important, places like Hispaniola provided a staging area for further explorations on the mainland, and it was from this vantage point that many a subsequent expedition was launched.

Newcomers to the Western Hemisphere found there groups of natives in varying stages of civilization. Columbus described the first ones he saw as being neither black nor white, but "the color of the Canary Islanders." The primitiveness of their culture was demonstrated to him when he handed them swords. Grasping the blades in ignorance, they cut themselves. They had seen their first iron. Concluding that the natives would make fine servants, and fit subjects for Christianizing, he took six home with him.

The aboriginal Americans

On the mainland there were larger groups of what the Spaniards called Indians. Such tribes as the Aztecs of Mexico and the Incas of Peru had a remarkably advanced political and economic organization. Instead of making the task of conquest harder, their civilization simplified it, for the Spanish, by controlling the leaders, easily subjugated the others. Later on, the English in North America would find the task of suppressing the wilder tribes a long and arduous one.

Each of the hundreds of tribes of American Indians had evolved its own culture in response to the demands and the resources of the environment in which it lived. The European was puzzled by the American Indian, and by his cultures, in which the complex and the primitive existed side by side. The Indian made beautiful baskets and pottery, skillfully decorated clothing of animal skins and fine cotton cloth, jewelry of shell and hammered silver and gold, elaborate houses and huge temples. Yet because he had never learned to make metal tools, he was limited to simple ones of stone, wood, bone, or shell. For transportation he had canoes, toboggans, and snowshoes, but he had never used the wheel.

To the sailors who had lived for weeks on ship's fare, the abundant food of the New World may have seemed more of a reward for crossing the ocean than the gold ingots and precious jewels. The Indians introduced the white man to strange and delicious edibles, many of which he promptly adopted. White potatoes and sweet potatoes, corn, squash, melons, pumpkins, kidney beans and Lima beans, chili peppers, avocados, pine-apples, tomatoes, and peanuts went to Spain with the other spoils of the Americas.

The conquistador was the first white man to enjoy tobacco; to drink chocolate (from the cacao bean), the sacred drink of the Aztec Indians; to hear of the miracle cures wrought by quinine; and to taste vanilla. He saw the Indians playing a game with a resilient ball, which they made out of the milky sap of certain plants. This was Europe's introduction to rubber.

Obviously the American native was wholly unprepared for the arrival of the European. For centuries he had

In Peru, in 1532, the emperor of the Incas, Atahualpa, was carried on a golden throne to the camp of Pizarro, the Spanish explorer. When the emperor refused conversion to Christianity, the Spaniards began the slaughter depicted below.

enjoyed complete isolation and had not even suspected the existence of a place like Europe. During this time each of the native tribes had assumed control of a relatively small area of land and then settled down to rule it, knowing little of the adjacent country.

The Spanish especially had little difficulty in conquering South and Central America. The Indians were pleased to have European assistance in fighting their neighbors and welcomed the firearms, which gave them a vast superiority over their enemies, who knew nothing of such magic. Thus the Spanish did not have to divide and conquer. The natives were perfectly willing to fight one another, and before long the conquistadors, as the newcomers were called, controlled the land from Mexico to Patagonia. From then on it was a process of degradation for the Indian, either through enforced labor or the white man's vices and diseases, like liquor and smallpox. The same would be true of tribes in what is presently the United States, except that the process would be much slower.

The impact of America

The discovery by Columbus meant, in many ways, the rejuvenation of the Old World. In 1492, before the news of the rich new lands to the west brought visions of gold and adventure, the new century had been awaited with little hope. Medieval Europe, with its feudalism and its craft guilds, its monolithic Church and religion-dom-inated art and learning, was crumbling. The Church was being attacked on all sides. The fight against the infidel seemed hopeless; Constantinople had fallen to the Turks in 1453 and efforts to retrieve it for Christendom had failed. England and France had devoted the first half of the 15th century to fighting each other, the second half to trying to quash their powerful nobles. Spain as a nation had only just emerged out of loosely knit provinces. Except for the work of the Portuguese, there had been no significant break-through in geographic discovery for nearly a century.

Within a few years, however, the picture began to change. Stronger monarchs stamped out local opposition and proceeded determinedly on a course of nationalistic expansion. Now, with the Americas open and waiting for exploitation, the energies of Europe could be directed across the Atlantic. As an immediate revivifier, huge amounts of gold and silver began to flow through the economic arteries and the greatest boom Europe had ever known had started.

Now the westward rush was on. No respectable nation could be without its colony from which it could gain bullion and raw materials and in which it hoped to dispose of surplus manufactured materials. Like the eastern United States in later gold-rush days, Europe took full advantage of the virgin land to the west. For the next 400 years this was to be the story of America.

THE SPANISH CONQUEST

"I discovered many islands inhabited by people without number; and I took possession of them all for Their Highnesses, by proclamation and hoisting the Royal Standard." Thus wrote Christopher Columbus to the court of Ferdinand and Isabella, reporting on one of history's most fateful voyages. He had touched and probed a New World of unimaginable riches and an unimaginable destiny, and he had stamped it with the seal of Spain. It was Spain that would find and seize and build upon the islands of the Caribbean, the fabulous kingdoms of Mexico and Central America, the rich fringes of the continent to the south and lands in the sea to the west. She would put down enduring roots in California and in what was to become the southwestern corner of the United States. With Spain more than with any other European nation, the opening of our hemisphere is identified. Her record of conquest in the New World was a patch-quilt of motives. Cruelty there was, and heroism; lust and sanctity; the desire to uplift and the greed to exploit. In the 1600 engraving (above), an Indian chief, angered by the quarreling of greedy conquistadors, contemptuously strikes down the tribute scales.

23

THE NIÑA'S PILOT
MAKES A MAP

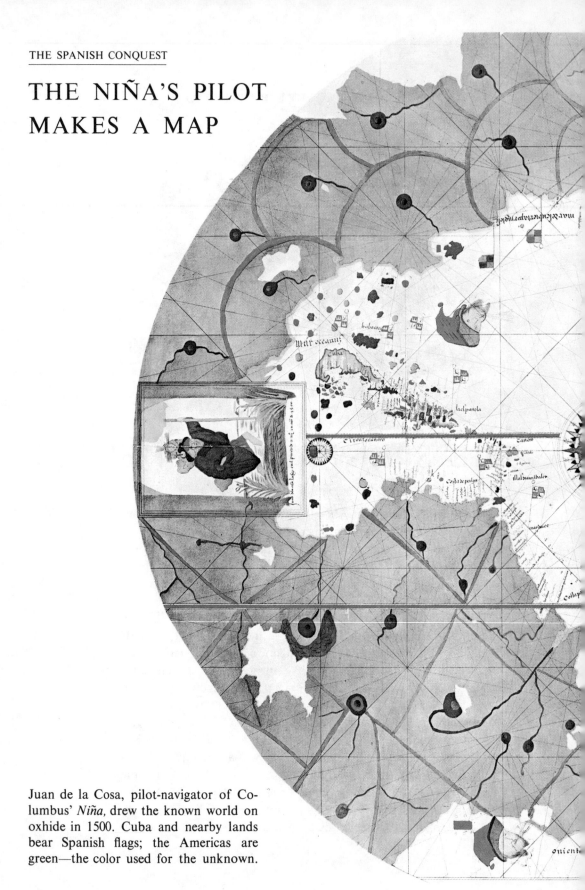

Juan de la Cosa, pilot-navigator of Columbus' *Niña,* drew the known world on oxhide in 1500. Cuba and nearby lands bear Spanish flags; the Americas are green—the color used for the unknown.

Left: Aztecs store food against famine—a real danger in drought-prone Mexico. Aztec slaves (right), often prisoners of war, sometimes sold their own children into bondage.

THE SPANISH CONQUEST

BEFORE THE SPANISH CAME

The conquistadors were often cruel and grasping, but the realities of Indian life itself—slavery, cannibalism, ruthless slaughter in war—were grim enough. On the opposite page is an Aztec tribute roll. Bordering glyphs at left and bottom represent conquered cities. Across the top are blankets of varying designs; the tree symbol meant 400 blankets of that type were to be paid. Below these are the other objects that were exacted as payment from the many subject peoples.

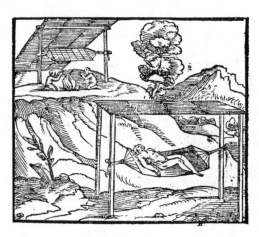

A contrast to the inventive Aztecs were the Caribs (left), cannibal fishermen of the islands. Primitive Venezuelans (right) invented the hammock; Spaniards soon copied it.

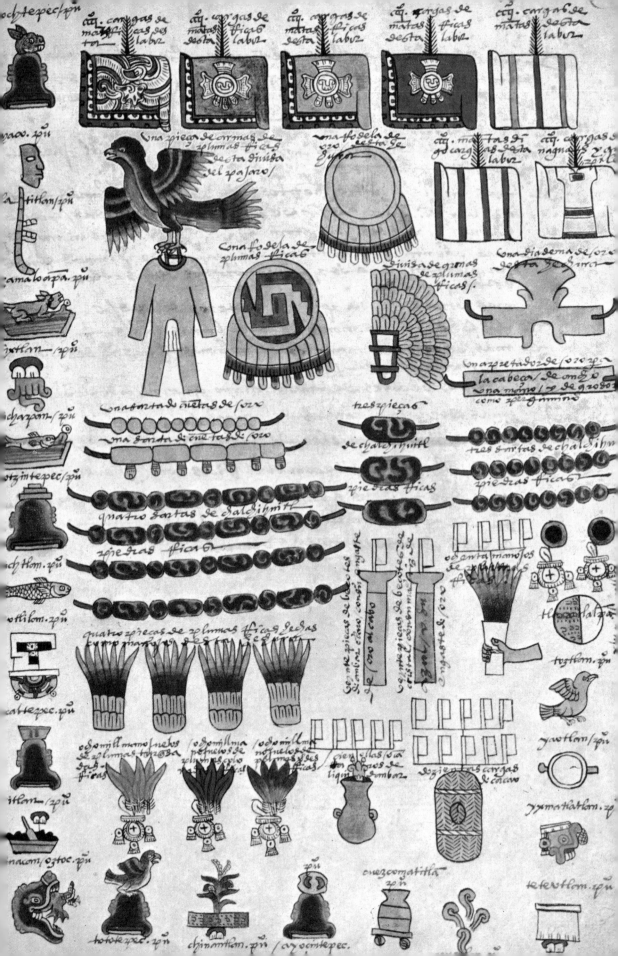

GREAT CITIES, DRENCHED IN BLOOD

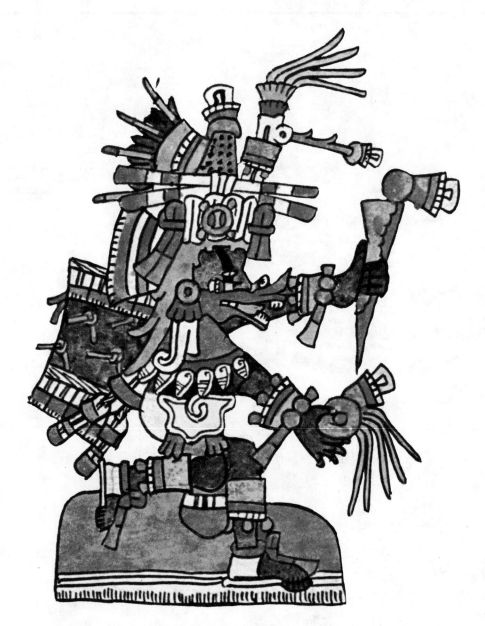

Above: As drums beat, Aztec priests lead victims up a pyramid to the temple to be sacrificed. Aztecs believed that unless the state god Huitzilopochtli were appeased by human blood, the sun would fail.

Right: An Aztec priest, having cut the heart from a living victim, offers it to the sun god Tonatiuh. The Spaniards found 136,000 human skulls at the temple in Tenochtitlán, modern Mexico City.

Opposite page: Quetzalcoatl, god of the morning star, played a part in the conquest of Mexico. Aztecs believed he was white and would return one day; when Hernando Cortez arrived, they at first welcomed him, mistaking him for the god.

In April of 1519, Hernando Cortez landed 600 soldiers on the east coast of Mexico, burned his boats so none could turn back, and went to Tenochtitlán, gleaming capital of the Aztec empire. Half believing that Cortez was Quetzalcoatl, the emperor Montezuma—represented (left) by the feathered glyph beneath his near-nude messenger—sent gifts to halt the attack. Instead, Cortez took Montezuma into custody while his troops took the city. Revolt flared, and in 1521 they had to retake it. Cortez himself, wounded, had to be fished out of a canal by a native ally (above). With a ridiculously tiny army he had conquered a land larger than Spain, and one brimming with wealth.

THE SPANISH CONQUEST

THE WHITE GOD COMES TO CONQUER

THE VICTORS' SPOILS

The Spanish acquired huge wealth from the Indians' rich treasuries or from the mines that they operated, such as the large one (above) in Potosi, in what is now Bolivia. In this 1584 picture, the raw metal is brought by llamas to the refinery (foreground) to be processed.

BRITISH MUSEUM, LONDON

An example of the Spaniards' brutal treatment of the Indians is shown above in a painting from an Aztec petition of 1570.

PONIENTE

Tollae...

JOHN CARTER BROWN LIBRARY

Silver ore is being smelted in Mexico in the picture at the right. It was painted by Samuel de Champlain between 1599–1602.

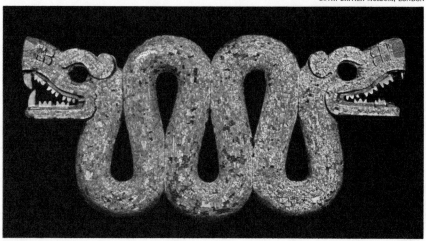

Among the beautiful objects brought home by the conquistadors was a 17½-inch-long ornament of shell and turquoise, perhaps an Aztec fire serpent.

THE SPANISH CONQUEST

THE WEALTH OF THE INDIES

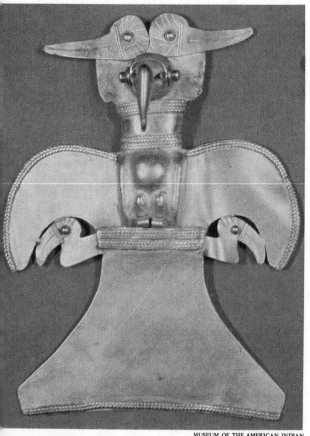

In 1520, the German engraver Albrecht Durer, viewing the presents sent by Montezuma to Charles I, described in his diary "an entire golden sun a full fathom wide, and likewise an entire silver moon equally as large . . . and all sorts of marvelous objects . . . much more beautiful than things spoken of in fairy tales." It is impossible to put a price upon the total booty of the conquistadors. Montezuma's treasures alone were valued by the historian Prescott at $6,000,000. Another 19th-century scholar said the roomful of gold that the perfidious Pizarro demanded for Atahualpa's ransom was worth $20,000,000. And of course there was, in the fabulously rich mines, more where that wealth came from. The gold ornament (left) is from Colombia. The skull (right), overlaid with obsidian and turquoise, probably represents the somber Aztec god Tezcatlipoca.

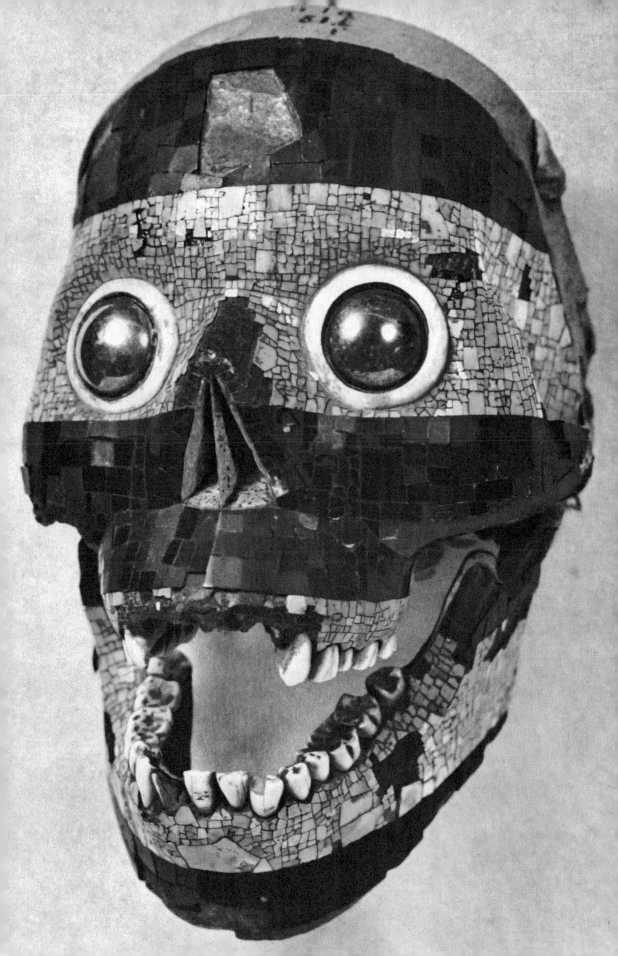

CHAPTER 2

COLONIES FOR ALL

By 1492 there was little evidence to suggest Spain was ready to embark upon worldwide exploration and conquest. The residents of that country had struggled for over 700 years to fight off the incursions of the Moslems, who had invaded in 711. During these bloody centuries, attention was paid wholly to internal affairs; there was hardly a moment to look abroad. In 1402, Henry III of Castile had sent out a small expedition to take control of the offshore Canary Islands, but due to pressures at home no real colonial effort resulted. Such projects were set aside for another 90 years.

Events moved rapidly in 1492, however, and by the middle of that year hopes for expansion were much stronger. The Moslems now were confined to a small area in the southern part of the country, known as Granada, and soon they would be evicted. Already the two principal monarchies of the peninsula were joined in a family union through the marriage of

A Timucua chief in Florida consoles the wives of warriors killed in battle. From a 16th-century eyewitness drawing.

Ferdinand of Aragon and Isabella of Castile. For the time being, each province maintained its own governmental structure, but that distinction would go. With the triumph over the Moors, a large number of unemployed soldiers, hardened from years of campaigning and restless for further excitement, were eager to join in any adventure that might promise fortunes. Reports of breath-taking opportunities in the lands Columbus had discovered gave a driving force from within Spain that sent legions of adventurers out on missions of conquest. With a more centralized government, supported by a strong Church, the country was ready to support such individuals. Powered by economic and religious forces, the expansion was bound to bring results.

Within a few years, individual names stood out on the roster of Spanish conquest. The adventures of Hernando Cortez became a legend. He entered Mexico in 1519, and after founding Vera Cruz, quickly fought his way to Mexico City. When that bastion fell, he conquered nearby territory and by 1522 reached the Pacific. While this was happening, Ferdinand

A 16th-century water color shows the army of Cortez marching on Mexico City.

Magellan's fleet not only crossed this great body of water but sailed completely around the world. Vasco de Balboa found the Pacific in 1513 by crossing the Isthmus of Panama, thus providing an entering wedge for Spanish expansion in that area. A little before Cortez was establishing himself firmly in Mexico City and Magellan was on the high seas, Ponce de Leon made the first of his explorations into Florida, in search—as legend claims —of waters reputed to have marvelous powers of rejuvenation. He received an arrow wound on his last trip there and returned to Cuba in 1521 to die. Others carried on his work. In 1528, Cabeza de Vaca moved along the Florida coast and then sailed across the gulf to present Texas, where most of the party was lost. De Vaca and three others turned up years later in Mexico, where they reported the fabulous Seven Cities of Cibola and their gleaming walls. Between the years 1539 and 1543, Hernando De Soto's exploring party of 500 men scoured the present Southeastern states in search of treasure. They found little of material value but gained much geographical knowledge. De Soto died in 1542 as his party descended the Mississippi River, and more than a year later the remnants of the expedition straggled into Mexico.

Accounts brought back by the conquistadors generated further attempts.

The tales arising from de Vaca's journey, for example, so excited the imagination of those at Mexico City that in 1539 a Franciscan friar named Fray Marcos de Niza was sent out with de Vaca's companion Estevanico to investigate. Due to a hostile reception by the Indians, they failed to locate the Seven Cities, but reports of their journey were so exaggerated that in 1540 Francisco Coronado was dispatched upon yet another expedition in the same region. After marching for two years through parts of present Arizona, New Mexico, Kansas, and the Texas Panhandle, this latest adventurer returned, thoroughly disappointed. He found no "fishes as big as horses" or natives whose kitchenware was made of gold, as his guide had promised. But even though he discovered no cities of silver, Spanish geographical knowledge and land claims were increased.

While the various expeditions were being carried on in North America during the years 1520 to 1540, there was an equally feverish search going on in South America. After several unsuccessful attempts to conquer Peru, Francisco Pizarro gained control in 1533. During the next three years he consolidated his gains, with the result that huge amounts of bullion were sent back to Spain. Unfortunately, in Peru, as was true in many other Spanish-conquered areas, the victors fell to fighting among themselves for supremacy, and the early days of the new regime were characterized by internal strife.

Control through monopoly

To achieve any real success in controlling its vast new empire, Spain had to evolve some kind of policy for governing it. One of the first problems confronting the conquistadors was that of the Indian. Historically the Spanish had treated any non-Europeans as barbarians and fit subjects for slavery, and it was not unnatural that Columbus should have taken home some of the natives in bond-

Aztec gold jewelry, including serpent, monkey, owl, and the head of a god.

age. Ferdinand and Isabella decided to take another course with regard to the New World and promised that the Indians would not only be treated kindly but converted to Catholicism. They freed the slaves that Columbus had taken.

It was at Hispaniola (Haiti), the first Spanish colony, that the new system of conversion was put into operation. The natives were divided among the colonists who were to Christianize them and to care for them. This division, which became known as the *repartimiento* (apportionment) system, actually resulted in slavery—although the crown continued to insist that even though the Indians were employed in such a manner, they were free. Isabella seemingly was more interested in the souls of the natives than their earthly existence. Upon her death the more practical Ferdinand came to power, and henceforth the exploitation was open and ruthless. It is not surprising that the result was a sharp rise in the death rate of those who were undergoing the rigors of being "saved."

Aside from control of the native population, the Spanish government lost no time in assuring itself that no other country would share in the exploitation of its newfound wealth. Each ship sailing from Spain carried instructions for collecting all available information for the king. All the mineral resources of the Americas were claimed by the crown. Individuals could work the mineral-bearing lands, but the monarch claimed half, or in some cases one-third, of the yield. However, gold and silver were not considered the only wealth to be realized, and at an early date colonists were urged to take along agricultural tools and seeds. The result was the introduction of wheat, barley, rice, sugar, lemons, olives, grapes, and other products into the Western Hemisphere. Cattle were brought here as early as 1494.

Transportation, another monopoly, was controlled by the use of a fleet of ships that plied back and forth across the Atlantic. It was known as the *flota,* and sailing twice a year with from 40 to 70 ships, this great convoy carried manufactures to America and returned with bullion or raw materials. No other country was allowed any trade with Hispanic America, and a rigid check was kept upon even the licensed traders.

Heretics were kept at home

To guarantee absolute economic control, there was organized in 1503 the *Casa de Contratacíon* (House of Trade). It acted as a funnel through which all goods passing between Spain and America, east or west, must go. Ultimately it came to control even human cargo and had the power to say who might go to the colonies. Only the faithful, the most sincere Catholics, were permitted to leave, for there were to be no religious heretics in the new land. Such stringent regulations were necessary if the

*These West Indies natives were first offered the opportunity to convert to
Christianity, and when they refused, they were mercilessly burned to death.*

little nation of Spain, having but
7,000,000 to 8,000,000 people, was to
conquer and exercise control over so
vast an area as Hispanic America.

The House of Trade worked well
enough in bottling up economic poten-
tialities abroad, but so vast was the
colonial undertaking that before long
some means had to be devised to keep
an eye on the rapidly spreading political structure. In 1524, therefore,
Charles I assented to the reorganiza-
tion of the Council of the Indies. This
small board carefully chose every offi-

41

In 1564, Le Moyne, a Frenchman, painted these Florida Indians. He discovered a column with French arms, planted in 1562 and worshiped by the Indians.

cial who was to go to America and kept a close check upon all those who went.

In addition to the Council of the Indies, the crown received help in administrative affairs abroad from representatives directly responsible to the king. These men, called viceroys, were absolute in America. Antonio de Mendoza, the first of them, took office in Mexico in 1535. The viceroy commanded immense respect and obedience and was so powerful that colonial residents were obliged to stand in awe of him, as if he were himself a king. On the economic side, this official was the king's watchdog, and he regularly visited the towns under his command to determine if more revenue could be produced or to see if any hidden treasure was escaping notice. Under him was an officer known as the captain general, who commanded the various subdivisions or districts within the viceroyalty. Although just a petty viceroy, he often communicated directly with the Council of the Indies to provide a check on the activities of his superior. To complete the circle, there was a local court known as the *audiencia*. It comprised usually three judges. This body kept an eye on both the viceroy and captains general and reported any suspicious activities to the monarch himself.

Spanish colonial administration was characterized by extreme control, which helps account for the fact that Spain had colonies in America longer than most of its European neighbors. It also explains in part why once the colonies of Spain had freed themselves, they had difficulty in establishing stable, self-sustaining governments. So long a time under such rigid and centralized control killed much of the initiative seen in the English colonies, where a measure of self-government existed from the outset.

France falls far behind

During the rich years of colonial adventure in the 16th century, when Spain established herself so firmly in the Western Hemisphere, France accomplished little. The French kings of that period desperately fought for complete authority at home and spent so much energy that any effort in America was out of the question. As if the internal difficulties were not enough, the French were unable to resist the lure of an apparently weak but rich Italy, and time after time their troops plunged southward into the peninsula, only to be hurled back. By 1600 the nation was bled dry and bankrupt. It was a sorry country that Henry IV took over in 1589. Roads were in disrepair, bridges destroyed, towns burned or abandoned, and the countryside teemed with plundering soldiers. Thus France was able to do little in America before 1600.

Despite the local turmoil and an inability to exploit colonial finds, and in face of the Spanish protest that the Pope had assigned to them the Western Hemisphere, there were some discoveries and claims made by the French during the apparently fruitless century. Between 1523 and 1543, men like Giovanni da Verrazano and Jacques Cartier carried the flag to North America, and in the two decades that followed, others attempted to found colonies as far south as Florida. When Henry IV came to power, his government at once showed a renewed interest in colonization. French capitalists could now turn their money toward American furs with royal encouragement. Between 1603 and 1615, Samuel de Champlain, the chief founder of New France, made many explorations, and in 1627 helped persuade Cardinal Richelieu, the power behind the French throne, to organize The Hundred Associates, a fur-trading monopoly. As part of the bargain, the company was to transport 4,000 agricultural settlers to the New World within 15 years.

The project was a failure. French Protestants were not allowed to leave the country, and the Catholics, who could, were reluctant. Unlike Spain, there was good farming land yet in France and hence little attraction for farmers in America. The peasant, despite his other difficulties, was attached to his land, and other pressures were not great enough to move him. So the French continued to be interested primarily in furs and not farms in the new country. By 1665 they had only about 3,500 settlers in America as compared to at least 75,000 English.

When Louis XIV, at 23, became the warlike despot of France in 1661, there was a renewed effort at colonization, despite the earlier failure of Richelieu. An earnest effort to gain something useful for the homeland, other than furs, was started. Jean Baptiste Colbert, the king's able minister of finance, tried to copy the English practice of developing colonies as a source of raw materials. The move fitted well into the current theory of economics known as mercantilism. According to that system, each nation tried to gain more gold than it found necessary to spend. Money, as always, was power, and the monarchs sought it ceaselessly. Colonies were regarded as a source of raw materials that could be processed in the mother country and the finished product sold at a profit, thus increasing the nation's supply of bullion.

Under Colbert's guidance, France

*New France became a valuable colony
17th-century print—fish caught off the*

pursued a policy of restrictiveness similar to that used by the Spanish—excluding foreigners from her colonial commerce and granting monopolies to merchants at home. The scheme worked fairly well in the West Indies. French-made goods were exchanged for tobacco, sugar, cotton, indigo, and other products not raised at home. Settlers in New France were expected to buy from France and in

for the reasons illustrated in this
coast and furs the forests yielded.

turn supply food, lumber, work animals, and other items of trade to the
West Indies. Here the plan broke
down and the French in the islands
were obliged to buy from the English.
To stimulate the lagging agricultural
efforts in Canada, the French now
tried to copy the Spanish system of
granting large blocks of land to enterprising individuals. However, unlike the Spanish, who were used to

living under feudalism, with the sei-
gneurs extracting rent and services
from their countrymen, few Frenchmen wanted to exchange a position
of relative freedom to return to feudalism, in America or anywhere else.

The colonial system of New France
also resembled the pattern set by
Spain in its type of government. It
was one of centralized control, with
the governor-general heading not only
the armed forces but also civil and
diplomatic departments. The familiar
system of cross-checks was provided
in the intendant, who acted as the
king's spy and kept him informed of
every development in the colony. In
addition, New France had a council
made up of the governor-general, the
intendant, the bishop of the Church,
and five (later 12) councilors appointed by the king. It issued all manner of decrees and was the court of
highest appeal in all the French possessions on this side of the Atlantic.

It was quickly apparent that the
French system was cursed by the same
restrictiveness as that of the Spanish. While it may have been successful
in driving off real interlopers, it had
a deadening effect that prevented a
real and constructive growth. All as-
pects of daily life were minutely regu-
lated. Besides the trade monopoly
enforced by the mother country, there
were rules concerning contact between the Indians and whites as well
as other personal curbs. As if the
governmental controls were not
enough, the clergy held a tight rein

45

This Dutch map of 1635 shows the Noord Rivier (the Hudson River), which Henry Hudson sailed up in 1609, seeking the Northwest Passage to the Orient.

over the colonists' moral and religious life. Here, as in New Spain, it was the business of the Church to see that no taint of heresy appeared. Under such scrutiny many a colonist decided to move westward, away from control and restriction. The population was too sparse to permit much spread, and in the end the process weakened New France.

Late as they were in the business of expansion, the French, like the Spanish, gained control of a large area. But they were unable to dominate it so well. The northern Indian tribes were nomadic, decentralized, and devoid of a form of government like that seen in Central America. The absorption of large groups of these Indians was a physical impossibility. Nor were economic opportunities so great as in South America. The Indians had no large amount of treasure, the climate was cold, and the variety of near-tropical products available farther south could not be produced here. Faced by vast distances, a forbidding land, and poor transportation facilities, the French came by a sprawling empire that produced little for them. Their total impression upon the New World, therefore, was considerably less than that of the Spanish or the English.

Unsuccessful imitators

In North America it was the English, and not the French or other European powers, who finally became dominant. The main challenge to the final winner came from four great Continental powers—Spain, France, Holland, and Sweden. While the French held a shaky grip on Canada, and Spain pushed up from the south, it was the Dutch who posed an immediate threat by planting a colony right in the middle of England's holdings. Holland, a rising commercial country in the 17th century, sent Henry Hudson on the same quest that all others sooner or later embarked upon —the discovery of a waterway across North America. In 1609 he sailed up a broad and encouraging-looking river that was to carry his name, and while he did not come out on the Pacific, he did lay claim to an important section of land. By 1624, the Dutch West India Company had dispatched people to America, and settlement of the Hudson River Valley had begun. Like the French, the Dutch were admittedly interested in the fur trade. New Amsterdam (New York) was established on the coast and Fort Orange (Albany) was built upriver as a fur-trading outpost. Flanked by forts on the Delaware and Connecticut Rivers,

Hudson went with his ship, the Half Moon, *for 150 miles up the river bearing his name. The Indians (below), seen staring at his ship, greeted him with generosity and traded beaver and otter skins for beads, knives, and hatchets.*

a small colonial empire made ready to establish a lucrative trade in valuable pelts.

During its existence of only 40 years, New Netherland grew slowly. It was hard to get Dutch burghers to leave comfortable homes in Holland. Blessed with religious toleration and a favorable agricultural system, few wanted to exchange them for life under the managers of large estates in America. The land system here, somewhat like that of Spain and France, featured control by aristocrats called patroons. They ruled over European tenants who worked the land. Despite the unpopularity of the system, it left its mark upon the American scene by establishing a social cleavage in New York that remained powerful until the 1830s. Like the French and Spanish systems, that of the Dutch was restrictive and centralized, allowing for little self-government. Officials sent out from Holland were superimposed upon the people, and organizations like the Dutch West India Company exercised far more control than many an emigrant liked.

As the Dutch colony struggled for a permanent place, nestled dangerously in English territory, the Swedes attempted to establish themselves on the shores of Delaware Bay. Fort Christina was built in 1638 on the site of present Wilmington. The colony never amounted to over 400, and in 1655 the Dutch conquered it. Within 10 years (by 1664) the English in turn took over the Dutch holdings and then turned on France.

America—a pawn of Europe

The American colonies of various European powers were pawns in a larger game. As the mercantile system developed, intense commercial rivalries grew in Europe, and the result was a race for power both at home and abroad. The long-range result was the weakening of the home government and an inability to press its colonial efforts further. Small but determined England gradually forged ahead in the contest with Spain, checkmating her more successfully than any other nation did. And even in Hispanic America there were great inroads made by the hard-fighting Elizabethan English, who by open war or covert smuggling chipped away at the Spanish holdings.

Of the several European powers holding to the theory of strict colonial control, Spain was best able to maintain its position in America. One by one, Sweden, Holland, and France lost out. But even the Spanish, with a complex and highly restrictive system, could not keep ideas from filtering into their colonies. Rule by arbitrary monarchs in a faraway land was hard to fix firmly upon an enormous American empire. When these distant kings fought one another at home and involved their colonies in expensive wars, the possibility of cutting loose from home ties became increasingly attractive to men in America.

PITKIN PICTORIALS LTD.

THE PILGRIMS' EUROPE

England at the turn of the 17th century was a land of sharp contrasts. Great wealth came to some people from the new and booming colonial trade; abject poverty came to others with the collapse of the feudal landholding system. The Church of England was opposed by the rebellious new Protestant sects that wanted to worship in their own way. Under Queen Elizabeth (above) the island kingdom became a colonial and merchant nation. Her successor, James I, who ruled from 1603 to 1625, failed to improve the lot of his subjects in the rural areas and also denied even the modicum of religious freedom Elizabeth had tolerated. It was during his reign that the Separatists—largely country people opposed to the state church—made their pilgrimage to Holland and then to America. Scenes of the England they left, and the Holland where they first sought refuge, are illustrated in this portfolio.

ELIZABETHAN LONDON

In the Pilgrims' day, London Bridge—shown above in 1639—was a bustling center for merchants and craftsmen. Goods from many distant lands were sold in the shops that lined the bridge, and the traders were eager for new markets. Seventy Merchant Adventurers from this section formed the company that financed the voyage of the Pilgrims.

The Englishmen at the right played major roles in the life of William Brewster, the Pilgrim who acted as religious leader of the Plymouth Colony. As a boy of 16, Brewster worked as a valet to Sir William Davison, a diplomat at the court of Queen Elizabeth. Both Brewster and his father worked for the family of Sir Edwin Sandys, who did much to help the Separatists gain permission to colonize.

SIR EDWIN SANDYS

SIR WILLIAM DAVISON

THE PILGRIMS' EUROPE

MERRIE ENGLAND

The England that the Separatists were so eager to leave behind had its gay and happy moments, as seen in this 1590 painting, *Wedding Feast at Bermondsey,* by Joris Hoefnagel. The building in the background, across the Thames, is the famous Tower of London.

RURAL
BEGINNINGS

The Separatist movement began in the peaceful English countryside, and some of its historic landmarks can be seen there today. William Bradford, who was to be governor of the Plymouth Colony, was born at Austerfield in an old stone farmhouse (right). While still a boy, he turned against the Church of England practices in the Austerfield parish church (above); instead he attended the unconventional services of Richard Clyfton in nearby Babworth. Clyfton, who was to shape Bradford's religious thinking, led a handful of country people in the kind of religious observance that was to become the rule in the Plymouth Colony.

BOTH: JOHN BULMER

PILGRIM HALL.

William Brewster abandoned his parish church, St. Wilfred's in Scrooby (above), to go to the same services at Babworth that young Bradford attended. Brewster's job as postmaster of Scrooby Post House (foreground) was taken from him in 1607 because of his religious activities.

55

In this 16th-century cartoon, a Puritan minister, reading the Bible from a pulpit, has his beard tweaked by an opposing religionist.

THE PILGRIMS' EUROPE

RELIGIOUS PERSECUTION

The Anabaptiſt.   The Browniſt.

The Familiſt.   The Papiſt.

The Separatists who came to America were not the only people in opposition to the Church of England in the 17th century. Four groups at odds with the state church are shown (left) tossing the Bible in a blanket. Three radical Protestant sects—the Brownists, the Anabaptists, and the Familists—are included, as well as the Papists (Roman Catholics).

A Church of England gathering, held in the courtyard of London's St. Paul's Cathedral in 1618, is shown at the right. Government control and approval of the proceedings is indicated by the presence of King James I, with his family, in the elevated royal box in the center.

57

PERTH ASSEMBLY.

CONTAINING

1 The Proceedings thereof.
2 The Proofe of the Nullitie thereof.
3 Reasons presented thereto against the receiving the fiue new *Articles* imposed.
4 The oppositenesse of it to the proceedings and oath of the whole state of the Land. *An.* 1581.
5 Proofes of the unlawfulnesse of the said fiue Articles, *viz.* 1. Kneeling in the act of Receiving the Lords Supper. 2. Holy daies. 3. Bishopping. 4. Private Baptisme. 5. Private Communion.

EXOD. 20. 7.
Thou shalt not take the name of the Lord thy God in vaine, for the Lord will not hold him guiltlesse that taketh his name in vaine.

COLOS. 2. 8.
Beware left there be any that spoyle you through Philosophy & vain deceit, through the traditions of men, according to the rudiments of the World, and not of Chrift.

MDCXIX.

By August of 1608 all of William Brewster's stalwart little band of English Separatists had arrived in Holland, the strange new land shown in the winter scene above. The future Pilgrims enjoyed the novelty of the canals and windmills, but the Dutch language and customs were hard for them to learn or even to understand. William Brewster, who became a printer in Leyden, Holland, found himself again in trouble with the British authorities when he ran off the tract at the left. The *Perth Assembly* was an attack on King James I for trying to force the Scotch Presbyterians to accept the authority of the Church of England. In 1620, having finally got permission to establish a colony in the New World, the English Separatists left Holland in the *Speedwell* (right). They were setting sail on the first leg of a difficult journey to a land and life unknown to them.

REFUGE IN HOLLAND

At Plymouth (above), the Separatists from Holland joined with those recruited in England. With little hope of ever seeing their homeland again, they boarded the *Mayflower,* seen riding at anchor in the harbor.

THE PILGRIMS' EUROPE

ON TO AMERICA

The uncompromising, arrogant James I of England, seen at the left in his most elegant royal costume, was unwilling to allow his subjects to worship as they pleased. To the Puritans' demand for "liberty of conscience" he said, "I will make them conform themselves or I will harry them out of the land."

At the right is the only surviving and authentic known portrait of a passenger on the 1620 voyage of the *Mayflower*. It is a painting of Edward Winslow, who once worked with William Brewster at his press in Leyden. Winslow, founder of a famous New England family, sat for the artist during a visit to England in 1651.

61

ÆTATIS·SVÆ·34
ANNO·DOMINI·1588

CHAPTER 3

THE ENGLISH COLONIES

Anyone studying the expansion of European nations in America may ask, "Why did England succeed so admirably when she entered the colonial race so late?" The Portuguese were hard at work exploring more than 200 years before the Jamestown settlement was established in 1607. By that date the Spanish were thoroughly entrenched in the New World, spreading their power throughout South and Central America, Mexico, and well into the present southwestern United States. Sir Francis Drake circumnavigated the globe 50 years after Magellan showed the way. Even the French preceded the English in America by planting a colony at Port Royal, Nova Scotia, in 1605.

Historian Charles A. Beard suggested some of the answers. England, being an island, was protected from the ravages of European armies and could spend defense funds for a navy rather than a large army. This made it possible not only to defend the homeland but also to send ships far

Sir Walter Raleigh, poet and statesman under Elizabeth and James I, organized some of the early expeditions to America.

across the world to establish and protect colonies. At an early date England's naval power soared to worldwide notice. By 1588 it would sweep the Spanish invaders out of the English channel, and then set about chasing away the Dutch and bottling up the French navy.

Rivalries on the Continent were another factor that worked in favor of England. While Europeans pounded one another with body blows which resulted in a loss of men and resources, England stood aloof, preserving her strength and always holding the balance of power. As France futilely fought Holland (which received just enough English aid to fight back), thousands of French and Dutch soldiers died who might have been colonists. Further blood was let as France tore herself to pieces with the wars of religion in the latter half of the 16th century, fought with Spain over spoils in Italy, and participated in a general European quarrel known as the Thirty Years War. There was no possibility that Germany or Italy would try to colonize, for these countries as we know them did not exist until the 19th century. During the intervening years the organized nations of Europe fought over them in quest of spoils, while, in general, England looked on. From time to time the English participated, when and where it would avail them of something useful, but more often they stood back and watched their sister countries on the Continent undo themselves.

Another reason the English were successful in America was the inconsistency of their rivals. In particular the Dutch and French—both nations of shrewd traders—failed to make a unified effort in colonizing America. For a period of years they would work hard at it; then as wars broke out at home, the colonial effort would lag. Already mentioned is the fact that the French were narrow in their policies toward the colonies. Their refusal to let the Huguenots emigrate to the New World is illustrative. Spain was no less guilty. Despite initial economic success, it was essentially a feudal and clerical land. There was little manufacturing and almost no middle class to act as a commercial backbone. Like that of the French and Dutch, the Spanish policy was essentially restrictive and exploitive so far as America was concerned.

Were the English more successful than their rivals simply because of an abundance of sea power and an ability to exploit a political balance of power in Europe? There were other factors involved. The colonization of English North America was carried out by an essentially civilian group, privately financed and led by self-appointed administrators. It was the beginning of America's much talked-of private enterprise and rugged individualism of a later day. While it was more a corporate undertaking than individual, and was controlled by governmental regulations in England, there was less direct participation by the home government than in rival colonies.

The feminine influence

Another farsighted practice of the English was to bring along their women. This made for a more homogeneous society than that of the French and Spanish colonies, in which men took native wives. And it also meant the family unit was to provide a solid core for a racially well-knit people, who early indicated that they had come to stay. For the next 300 years, as the descendants of these early settlers pushed westward across the continent, building the nation, it was the presence of the women and of the unit that provided stability and permanence to the new communities. It was they who demanded schools, religion, and order. It was their presence that encouraged a cultural uplift and broke down some of the roughhouse tendencies of the masculine frontier. While the Spanish and French ranged over vast stretches of land, unhampered by any family ties, except momentary domesticity with occasional native women, the English

The English triumph over the Spanish Armada in 1588 put an end to the efforts of Philip II of Spain to annex England to his empire—by force or by marrying Elizabeth. This idealized portrait was painted after his death by Rubens.

65

Henry VIII

stayed close to home. The result was a family type of frontier, characterized by small farms, that remained much more compact, more easily defended, and permanent in nature.

If the colonial methods employed by England account for her success, her preparation at home for such a venture must not be overlooked. By 1600 she had moved farther away from the system of feudalism than any of her Continental neighbors. There was no dominant military clique, and the monopolistic clergy, once the owner of large land holdings, had been deprived of considerable power. As these forces diminished on the national scene, there arose a strong merchant class. It produced a number of small, independent capitalists, ready and willing to project their efforts anywhere in the world in search of profit.

A by-product of this business growth was the emergence of responsible government and constitutional law. The merchants, orderly and regular in their conduct, demanded the same from the government. An arbitrary monarch, always greedy for funds and accustomed to wielding the mace of taxation when and where he felt like it, could not be a part of this system. The merchant class demanded that the king be responsible to his government and made the demand stick. This group of businessmen were becoming more secular than religious in their thinking, more interested in the credit rating than the religious beliefs of their friends. Naturally the pressure of business interests tended to relax earlier religious intolerance.

In order to take advantage of worldwide commercial possibilities, Englishmen began to combine their assets in the form of trading companies. Corporate effort proved to be much more successful than individual attempts. In 1555, the first of the major English trading companies, the Muscovy Company, was chartered to trade with Russia. And in Elizabeth's reign, charters were granted to the Levant Company, which broke into the Italian trade monopoly of the Near

East, and to the East India Company, which stretched its tentacles to the Ganges in India, forcing its way into the Portuguese concessions there. Thus, when the possibility of planting a colony in North America presented itself, the English were quite at home in the formation of corporations for just such an adventure. With no difficulty the London Company and the Plymouth Company were organized in 1606.

Why Englishmen left home

If conditions in France, Holland, and Sweden were good enough to discourage people from exchanging their old homes for new, such was not the case in England. The disappearance of serfdom, gradual as it was, resulted in unemployment for thousands of peasants who had for years quietly farmed under the feudal system. The change did not necessarily arise out of humanitarian sentiments of the masters. The old system proved to be unprofitable in a money economy, and many a landlord was glad to free his land of the peasants who ate up his produce. The owners were eager to convert their lands into some kind of cash crop. Sheep raising had become popular as the demand for wool by Flemish weavers across the channel grew. Thousands of acres were now fenced off by hedges, and the great enclosures, as they were called, became the order of the day. Estates that had once employed large numbers of workers now needed only a few sheepherders; an unprecedented agricultural unemployment resulted.

To make it all worse, about this time a large amount of land was taken from the Catholic Church as Henry VIII broke with that institution. The new masters, bent upon making the greatest profit in the shortest time, enclosed the land and threw even more farmers out of work. Thus by the time of Elizabeth (1558) droves of unemployed roamed the highways. England's pauper population grew and debtors filled the prisons. The newly freed serfs found that their escape from bondage was a questionable boon, and any opportunity was

Flemish farmers in the 16th century were content to stay home and work in the fields.

taken to leave England. The price of a passage to America was to become an indentured servant, another type of bondage, but as there was little alternative, thousands went.

England's religious situation provided another, although less important, reason for moving. During the 1540s, Henry VIII had broken with the Catholic Church at Rome, and through the next 20 years there was a confused struggle to see if the nation would be predominantly Catholic or Protestant. At the time Elizabeth came to the throne, the answer appeared to be the latter. A few years later, with the adoption of the Thirty-nine Articles and certain supplementary measures, England became Anglican Protestant. Since the reign of Henry VIII, the church had been governed by an archbishop who received his appointment from the monarch, thus assuring governmental control of the religious hierarchy. Many Catholics believed that the newly established Church of England would bring no fundamental changes other than a physical separation from Rome. Indeed, the new church preserved a large part of the Catholic ritual and beliefs, modified only by a strong Calvinistic theological tinge.

As in every society, there were those who did not think the reforms far-reaching enough. They wanted to "purify" the church by eliminating more of the old Catholic ritual. They came to be called Puritans. Another group, the Separatists, more radical in

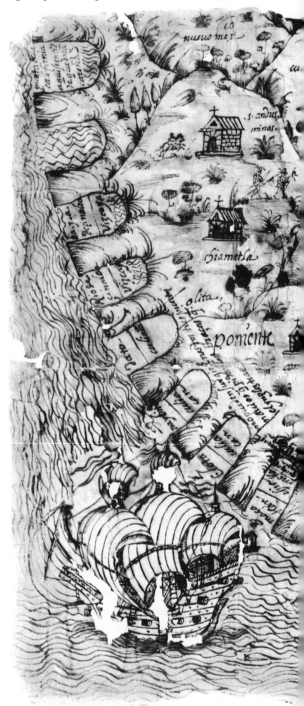

This 17th-century Spanish map shows the ports from Guatemala to California looted by Thomas Cavendish in 1587, along the path of Sir Francis Drake's raids in 1579.

belief than any of the others, wanted to get away completely from the notion of an established church. Both the Puritans and Separatists complained so much to King James I, in-sisting that they be allowed to worship in their own churches in their own way, that he lost his temper and announced that the dissidents must conform or be driven

Three English raiders—Sir John Hawkins, Sir Francis Drake, and Thomas Cavendish.

of today, commercial vessels could easily be converted into fighting ships by the addition of firepower and other modifications. By the reign of Elizabeth, England had already become a formidable sea power; that fact was demonstrated to the world when in 1588 the Spanish attempted to invade the British Isles.

Yet, while others were busy colonizing, Englishmen momentarily neglected claims made for them in America by such men as John Cabot. As the leading Protestant power, they seemed content to contest the claims of Catholic nations like Spain and Portugal. John Hawkins and Francis Drake led others in this naval hamstringing operation, striking continually at the Spanish monopoly in particular. Hawkins raided that preserve as early as 1562 by engaging in the slave trade and selling Negroes in Hispanic America in direct violation of the law that forbade the colonists to trade with any nation but Spain. Drake, another Protestant, regarded it his duty to lash out at Roman Catholic sovereigns, and under the guise of such a worthy cause he launched himself upon a semi-piratical career at sea. Spanish ships and seaports suffered heavily from his hit-and-run raids, and this was at a time when England and Spain were at peace. To punish him for such transgressions, Queen Elizabeth shared Drake's loot and made him a knight.

As the 17th century neared, England made ready to enter the colonial

from the land. Despite these blustering words, a law designed to stop the emigration of nonconformers had been in effect since 1598. All who wished to leave England must get a license from the king. But, in 1617, ailing Jamestown needed colonists so desperately that James I agreed to allow the Separatists to go to the New World. England, like her Continental neighbors, was also to have her heretics. But her desire to colonize the New World was more overriding than that of her neighbors.

One of the most important results of England's commercial growth was the emergence of a large and powerful fleet. In early times there was no great difference between men of war and merchantmen; unlike those

Queen Elizabeth's courtiers are shown carrying their unmarried ruler on a throne to the wedding of Anne Russell, one of her ladies in waiting.

game. In 1583, Sir Humphrey Gilbert sailed to America and tried to plant a colony at New Foundland. He hoped to start with a settlement along what was believed to be the Northwest Passage—the long-sought waterway to Asia—and thus gain commercial advantage on what would be a vital trade route. No doubt the fishermen, who had been drying fish there for possibly a hundred years, listened with surprise as Gilbert gravely read to them a patent issued by the queen that directed him to discover fresh lands. This ceremony over, he packed up a piece of New Foundland turf, formalizing his accomplishment, and headed for England. The adventurer was lost at sea on the way home and his rights reverted to a half brother,

Sir Walter Raleigh. In 1584 this more famous colonizer sent forth an exploring party that spent two summer months scouting the South Atlantic seaboard.

So favorable were the reports that in the following year 108 colonists crossed the Atlantic to take possession of "heathen lands" and to find gold. A most important section of the patent granting them permission to settle on Roanoke Island on Albemarle Sound extended the same privileges as those given to the Englishmen at home. The queen was so impressed by what she had heard of the new location that she suggested it be named Virginia after her, the "virgin queen." The new residents were somewhat less enthusiastic about the place, however,

71

and in 1586 when Sir Francis Drake stopped by to see how they were getting on, they all asked for and were granted passage home.

In 1587, another group, this time 116 in number, was sent back to Roanoke Island for a new try at establishing a permanent colony. Because of the Spanish Armada's attempt to storm the island bastion that was England, and for other reasons, no support reached the little settlement until 1591. The crew of the relief ship searched, but no sign of the settlers was found.

As the 16th century drew to a close, England had not yet established herself on the coast of North America. While colonizing in North Carolina lagged, new attempts were being made to the north. In 1605, Captain George Weymouth landed on the coast of Maine, hopeful of finding a suitable location, but he turned up nothing of interest except a few natives. Unwilling to go home empty-handed, he captured five of them, and before they reached England, he had taught them enough English to talk of the fine climate and rich resources in America. Few modern realtors could top this feat.

Despite such failures, men of England indicated a strong interest in the new land, and since their charters usually provided that Englishmen might carry their privileges and liberties abroad, further attempts were bound to follow. Materially, they had brought home only the white potato

and tobacco. Sir Ralph Lane, governor of Raleigh's first colony, introduced the potato to his Irish estate, and it was Raleigh himself who popularized smoking with the new brown leaf. Small as were these contributions, they were later to affect commercial Europe mightily. Meanwhile, Spain entered her second century of successful colonial adventure in America; already she was fabulously rich in silver and gold.

The failure of early efforts in Virginia indicated that the task was too big for individual enterprise. The hazards were too great and the cost too high. It was here that Englishmen,

The tattooed Florida warrior carries a quiver of arrows and a bow over six feet long.
BRITISH MUSEUM, LONDON

An engraving of John Smith, from his book about his 1614 New England voyage.

accustomed to sharing risks by corporate organization, successfully applied the method to America. Virginia presented a challenge to those at home; groups of merchants glimpsed opportunity abroad and were ready to act. The Spanish had found gold in America, and it was supposed that the English could also. But if bullion could not at once be uncovered, perhaps other wealth could be had by discovering a waterway across the continent. Innumerable river mouths along the coast looked promising. The government was willing to back any ventures along the Atlantic seaboard, for it was now prepared to contest Spain's claim to a large share of North America. Mercantile England was rapidly expanding, and the demand for raw materials grew daily. No European country except Holland was now more interested in a source of supply for its workshops. Great as

were the strides in commerce and industry, unemployment resulting from the enclosures mounted to a point where the government sought a place for its people to overflow. And for those who were unhappy over the religious differences at home, America would be a fine place, too.

Not until 1603 was there a real prospect that Virginia would at last become a permanent settlement. In that year Sir Walter Raleigh was stripped of his colonizing rights, and the way was cleared for a company to take over. When peace came with Spain in 1604, there was further stimulation for the venture. Two years later James I issued charters to two groups of merchants, authorizing them to establish two settlements in America, each of which would comprise 10,000 square miles of land. The Plymouth Company's preserve lay somewhere between latitudes 38°N. and 45°N., and the London Company was assigned the region between latitudes 34°N. and 41°N. In granting the charters, the government did not surrender the right to govern the colonies. A council, appointed by the king, was to sit in England and supervise, while a local council appointed by this body would carry on day-to-day affairs in America. The colonial council had to abide by English laws and was prohibited from passing laws affecting life and limb. Otherwise, it was self-governing. Under this arrangement, the English settlement of North America went ahead.

Powhatan appears in John Smith's 1631 edition of the Generall Historie of Virginia.

The London Company got a head start on the Plymouth Company and in 1607 established what would be the first permanent English town in the present United States. It was named Jamestown, in honor of the king, and American real estate got off to a fast start as John Smith avowed that "heaven and earth never agreed better to frame a place for man's habitation." The original 105 settlers would soon question this extravagant claim, but for the present they could do little but assault the many problems that faced them in the American wilderness.

Complexities of rooting a civilization on a virgin land soon became apparent. Along with the to-be-expected pioneer hardships, the Jamestown settler had to learn to live with the Indian. Powhatan, the powerful chief of the Algonquians, earnestly worked for peace with the Englishman, but Jamestown did suffer sneak attacks by one or another of the villages in Powhatan's confederacy. Yet, despite these sporadic uprisings (sometimes incited by the Spanish to the south), peaceful coexistence was the rule during the difficult early years of the Virginia colony.

As if the external troubles were not enough, however, the men of Jamestown had their own quarrels. The seven-man local council included such strong personalities as Edward-Maria Wingfield and John Smith, and their violent quarrels resulted in division and suffering for all residents. Even more threatening to the little settlement was the incidence of disease. So prevalent was sickness that despite the arrival of two additional groups of people in 1608, the population declined. When in January, 1608, a fire destroyed most of Jamestown's buildings and shortly thereafter rats devoured much of the remaining corn supply, the probability of a permanent settlement in America took a turn for the worse.

The "gentlemen" go on strike

Moreover, there were times when the settlers seemed to be working against their own interests. Some of them took the position that as "gentlemen" they should not work with the soil, but ought to spend their time looking around for precious metals. Some of the other gentlemen preferred not to engage in any labor at all. Meanwhile, in England, the London Company was overanxious for immediate monetary return. Twice during 1608, when vessels arrived in America, the colonists had to stop their building and supply lumber, pitch, tar, and other cargo for shipment home. Precious time was lost, and the much-needed preparations for protection against Indians and a long winter were delayed.

Before long there were loud protestations. Out of the bickering, and despite a number of examples of rugged individualism on the part of the settlers, John Smith managed to gain recognition as the leader. Under his guidance some of the gentlemen found themselves engaged in the ungentlemanly task of cutting down trees. Before long, blistered hands produced a variety of colorful oaths, which Smith answered with a decree that blasphemy would be punished by pouring a can of cold water down the offender's sleeve. While this may have cooled hot tempers, it resulted in more respect than love for the leader, and increased discontent.

Because of complaints from those in America and a fading interest in England, the company decided to liberalize the colony's government. Under a new charter of 1609, which greatly enlarged the colony's boundaries, residents were offered stock in

Sir John Popham financed expeditions, as a partner of Sir Ferdinando Gorges.

the company and given an opportunity to pay for it by labor. In addition to the new charter, more supplies were sent out. They were not enough, and Jamestown now faced the "starving time." Settlers were obliged to eat snails, snakes, roots—anything they could find. The crisis passed, and under more severe laws that demanded strict order, the faltering colony once again went forward. A third charter, issued in 1612, granted the London Company even more power to control its colonial project. If it could only find some profitable product to export from America, the whole scheme promised ultimate success. The search was rewarded by the development of tobacco, and with a cash crop for sale,

the Virginians announced they were in business.

While the London Company struggled to establish a colony in Virginia, those at Plymouth, England, had even less success. The land assigned to them lay north of Virginia, in a region devoid of treasure and less conducive to agricultural attempts. In 1607, Sir John Popham and Sir Ferdinando Gorges had tried to plant a colony on the mouth of the Kennebec River in Maine, to no avail. In 1610, a group of Bristol merchants, armed with a charter, sent a group of 39 colonists to New Foundland. Despite the fact that they landed at so promising a place as Cupid's Cove, on Conception Bay, there was no satisfactory population increase and the colony faltered.

Four years later some London merchants hired the well-known Captain John Smith, recently of Virginia, to hunt whales along the North Atlantic coast. While on this assignment he did a little exploring, and after returning home wrote a book called *A Description of New England,* wherein he coined a name. At once a best seller, the book created great excitement about this new land. Sir Ferdinando Gorges, a powerful member of the Plymouth Company, now applied to the king for a patent to explore and settle this much-talked-of area. In giving his permission, the monarch directed that the region be called New England; it lay between 40°N. and 48°N. latitude and extended from sea to sea.

Promoters in the London Company found their colonists in Holland, not in England. They knew that a group of English Separatists, living at Leyden, wanted to settle in America. Before long, one of the promoters, Thomas Weston, had persuaded the Pilgrims, as they became known, to accept his company's offer of trans-

portation to America and land when they arrived. After some delay they sailed, in September of 1620, along with a group of nondissenters who merely sought new homes in America. Just over 100 men, women, and children crowded aboard the *Mayflower*, and it was almost two months before they caught their first glimpse of America. On the trip there had been one death and one birth; the newcomer was appropriately called Oceanus. As the *Mayflower*'s passengers looked upon an arm of land that would be known as Cape Cod, they had reason to be thankful for a successful voyage. Considering the hazards of travel and crowded conditions, they had done well. So well, in fact, that it was decided they should land instead of searching farther southward for a better location.

First popular government

The decision to put ashore on the Massachusetts beach had some far-reaching implications for later Americans. Word spread throughout the ship's company that the landfall lay north of the jurisdiction staked out for the London Company and in effect they were in no man's land. Rather than being discouraged, some of the rougher elements of the London streets saw opportunity and announced that they would not be bound by the authority of the London Company. It was mutiny. The Pilgrim leaders acted promptly to quell such a premature declaration of independence. In solemn council they agreed

Massasoit

PILGRIM HALL

The first document in the New World to assure government by the rule of the
majority was the Mayflower Compact, signed on shipboard off the coast of
Cape Cod. Percy Moran painted this incident as it may have occurred.

on November 21 that they were now a body politic and that they would frame laws for the protection of their fellow colonists. In the Mayflower Compact, these men set up the first government of the people and by the people in America. Again and again, on later frontiers, men would sit together and formulate rules for temporary guidance until formal law reached them. The Pilgrim Fathers, like their successors, had no notion of political separation from the parent government; they were simply improvising in the face of necessity.

After preliminary explorations ashore, the colonists decided upon a location and named it Plymouth. On Christmas Day they began felling timber for the construction of buildings. By the early months of 1621, a common house flanked by a row of thatch-roofed huts made partly of woven brush and mud appeared on the shores of Plymouth harbor. Then one warm March day the Pilgrims had a visitor. An Indian named Samoset, wearing only a belt, strode into the village. In surprisingly good English (picked up from fishermen to the north), he welcomed the newcomers and promptly asked for beer. His wants satisfied, he disappeared. In a few days he returned with a friend named Squanto, who showed the hopeful farmers a few agricultural tricks. By fertilizing with fish the hills into which the corn kernels were planted, a better crop was assured. Before long the whites became acquainted with other natives,

and soon a fur trade sprang up. By fall a thriving commerce had been established and the corn stood high. Assisted by Chief Massasoit and his braves, the Pilgrims held the Thanksgiving feast so well known to Americans of today. After some years of exile in Holland, the little group of English Pilgrims had established themselves on raw and forbidding shores with less suffering than their countrymen at Jamestown had experienced. Before their establishment could be called permanent, however, there would be days of sickness and hunger.

Private enterprise proves itself

Like those colonists in Virginia, the Pilgrims at first tried a cooperative economic system, but within two years they abandoned it. In search of a method with more incentive, they turned to private enterprise, granting an acre of land to each man. The new plan worked well, and the harvest of 1623 was so rich that the first years of hunger were nearly forgotten. Four years later settlers bought out the London capitalists for 1,800 pounds, to be paid in nine installments, and freed themselves of financial control from England.

Between the years when settlements were first established at Jamestown and Plymouth, conditions in England made it desirable for many to seek homes elsewhere. In 1618 the Thirty Years War began on the Continent, and even though England was not at once involved, the turmoil had a powerful effect upon her expansion in the New World. As the economy experienced a shift-over from old farming methods to the raising of wool for sale in Europe, wartime conditions on the Continent began to hamper the sale of English cloth. With depression settling on the land, taxes became harder to bear and both farmers and

townsmen suffered. The Church grew increasingly insistent in its demands for religious conformity, to the annoyance of the already hard-pressed man on the street. Between 1618 and 1642 (when civil war broke out, making transportation hard to find), emigration from England grew to such proportions that these years are called the period of the great migration. Men and women left England in droves, headed for the mainland of America and also for the small islands in the Caribbean. Many of them were not people of great pioneering spirit and under normal conditions would have remained in their cottages, hopeful of better times. But these were *not* normal times, and the realization that they had nothing to lose and everything to gain sent them to the nearest seaports for passage. It was their resolve that strengthened the hold of the colonies along Atlantic shores.

The Ordeal of Cabeza de Vaca

A SPECIAL CONTRIBUTION BY

THOMAS F. McGANN

Shipwrecked on the coast of Texas in 1528, this indomitable Spanish explorer began an eight-year struggle for existence as he traveled through land unknown to the white man.

A crude boat carrying 40 exhausted Spaniards drifted close to the long Texas beach. "Near the land a breaker took and threw the boat the cast of a horseshoe out of the water. With the violent blow almost all the men, who were like dead, came to themselves and seeing the beach near they began to climb from the boat and crawl on hands and knees to some ravines where we made fire and toasted some corn that we had bought and drank some rain water that we found. The day that we arrived here was the sixth of the month of November." The year was 1528.

Thus Alvar Nuñez Cabeza de Vaca of Jerez, treasurer of the ill-fated Narvaez expedition, which had set out from Spain in June, 1527, with five ships and 600 men to explore and settle the lands between Florida and Mexico, tells how he came with his few remaining companions to the unknown land of Texas. Years before De Soto and Coronado entered what would become the United States, he was to make one of man's great land journeys, cross-

This Frederic Remington painting of de Vaca, bearded and seated between Indians, shows him in the arid land through which he traveled.

ing Texas and Mexico from the Gulf to the Pacific Ocean with two other white men and a black slave.

The Narvaez expedition had spent the winter of 1527–28 in Cuba and sailed in the spring for the little-known shores of Florida. On April 14—Holy Thursday—the five vessels anchored at the mouth of what was probably Tampa Bay. Here, the commander, Panfilo de Narvaez, made his most important decision, and so insured the destruction of his expedition. He divided his force, now only 400 men, took 300 of them ashore, and set out northward toward the place which the Indians called Apalache; there, they said, the Spaniards would find much gold. The ships were ordered to run along the coast and meet the men marching by land at a vague rendezvous. That rendezvous was never kept.

Narvaez and the others in the land party struggled along the coast of Florida, battling Indians all the while. When, late in June, they reached Apalache (perhaps near Tallahassee), the Spaniards found a few huts, corn, and hostile natives, but no gold. The invaders pushed inland, but hunger, sickness, and frequent attacks by the Indians made their march a nightmare.

In desperation Narvaez turned back to the coast and called a council. Cabeza writes, "We agreed on a remedy most difficult to execute, which was to make boats in which to depart . . . we knew not how to do this work, nor were there tools . . . but God willed it that one of the company should say that he could make

83

some wooden tubes which, with deerskins, would serve as bellows . . . and we agreed thus to make from our stirrups, spurs, and crossbows . . . the nails, saws, axes, and other tools of which there was such need. We agreed that every third day we would slaughter a horse to be divided among those working on the boats."

On September 20, five boats were ready, each 33 feet long. From palmetto fiber and the horses' tails and manes the men made rope and rigging, and from their shirts, sails. They flayed the horses' legs entire and tanned the skin to make water bottles.

Two days later, they ate the last horse. Leaving behind more than 50 companions, who had died of disease or wounds, some 250 survivors crowded into the vessels and sailed from the place they called the Bay of Horses.

The sea was as perilous as the land. The gunwales of the boats almost awash, their corn supply almost exhausted, the horsehide water carriers rotten and useless, the Spaniards groped westward along the coast, stopping to beg or to fight the Indians for fish and water. Maddened by thirst, some men drank salt water and died. One day the voyagers came to the mouth of a broad river whose current drove the boats away from the shore, but repaid the men with fresh water. It was the Mississippi.

The five boats were blown out to sea by a howling north wind and became separated. Cabeza and his men sailed for four days, until the roaring breakers hurled them upon the Texas shore that early day in November, 1528.

After the castaways had eaten what little corn they had salvaged, Cabeza ordered one of the men, Lope de Oviedo, to survey the country. When Oviedo returned, he reported they were on an island, and "three Indians with bows and arrows were following him and calling to him and he likewise was beckoning them on. Thus he arrived where we were, the Indians remaining a way back."

So, probably a few miles below the present city of Galveston, on a desolate island now joined to the mainland by the sea's powerful action and called Velasco Peninsula, Indians and white men met. This first meeting of Europeans and natives in the Southwest of the United States was peaceful. The Indians brought fish and roots to the starving strangers, receiving trinkets in return. After resting a few days, the Spaniards dug their boat out of the sand, and with much exertion launched it. Two crossbow shots from shore a wave capsized the boat, drowning three men and tossing the rest back upon the beach.

Here the Indians found them once more, and so sad was the plight of the white men that the Indians howled their ritual lamentation. The natives brought the castaways to their huts and warmed and fed them and then danced all night, to the terror of the Europeans, who feared that they were being prepared for sacrifice.

The next day some 50 more Spaniards came into camp. Led by Andres Dorantes and Alonso de Castillo, and including Dorantes' black slave, Estevanico, these survivors of the expedition had been wrecked a few miles further up the beach.

Together the Spaniards agreed to launch the boat of Dorantes and Castillo. The men who had the strength and will might go in it; the others would make their way along the shore.

The boat was launched, but it sank immediately. Marooned without provisions and with cold weather coming, the Spaniards decided to winter on the island. But they picked four men and sent them on down the coast in an effort to reach the Spanish settlements in Mexico.

Cold and stormy weather swept the island; the Indians could catch no fish and dig no roots; the flimsy huts gave no shelter; death came. Five Spaniards living apart in one hut became cannibals, "until only one remained who, being alone, there was no one who might eat him." Of the more than 80 Spaniards who had come to the island, soon only 15 remained alive.

The Spaniards named this place Malhado— Bad Luck Island. But with the help of the Indians, the 15 Europeans survived. These Indians went naked, except for "the women, who covered their bodies somewhat with a wool that grows in the trees." The men were large and well-formed; they pierced their lower lips and sometimes their nipples with

JOHN TEPPICH

Map labels: PROBABLE LOCATION OF THE TUNA GROUNDS WHERE CABEZA MADE HIS ESCAPE; TRINITY R.; BRAZOS R.; PECOS R.; COLORADO R.; GALVESTON ISLAND; CABEZA SHIPWRECKED; BIG BEND; "CORAZONES"; RIO SONORA; RIO GRANDE; NUECES R.; VELASCO PENINSULA; CABEZA SPENDS SIX YEARS AS AN INDIAN CAPTIVE, 1528-34; RIO SINALOA; SAN MIGUEL (CULIACÁN), Northernmost outpost of Spanish colonization on the west coast of Mexico; WHERE CABEZA MET THE SPANISH SLAVE HUNTERS, 1536; PÁNUCO (Nearest Spanish settlement and the goal of the Narváez Expedition's survivors); COMPOSTELA; MEXICO CITY; DESERT

SCALE
0   100   200   300   MILES
— · · · — MODERN U.S. STATE BOUNDARIES
■■■■■ CABEZA'S PROBABLE ROUTE

The precise route of Cabeza de Vaca is a puzzle in probabilities, and necessarily so because of the vagueness of the account of the principal witness, Cabeza himself. Many conflicting interpretations of his route exist, some of which are founded upon knowledge of the region and close analysis of Cabeza's narrative, others on local pride and supposition. An example of such controversy is whether or not Cabeza reached New Mexico and Arizona. Although he may indeed have wandered that far north, it now seems much more likely that he turned west somewhere below present-day El Paso. The route indicated on this map is the one considered most probable by the author of this article.

pieces of cane. They treated their children mildly, engaged in prolonged, lachrymose funeral rites, and had taboos against in-laws. Their beliefs involved the foreigners in a practice that was to save the lives of some of the hapless group: "They wished to make us physicians . . ." Cabeza writes. "They cure illness by blowing on the sick, and with that breath and the placing on of hands they cast out the sickness, and they ordered us to do the same and to be useful to them in some way. We laughed at that, telling them that it was a farce and that we did not know how to cure. For this they took away our food until we did as they told us. . . . The manner in which we cured was by blessing them and breathing on them and by praying a Pater Noster and an Ave Maria."

In the spring of 1529, the Spaniards separated. Thirteen survivors (one more had appeared in the winter) started off toward Mexico. Lope de Oviedo and Alaniz remained on Malhado, too weak to travel. Cabeza, who had been taken to the mainland during the winter and who had fallen ill there, also remained behind—the lone white man, as far as he knew, on the vast and unexplored mainland of North America above Mexico.

For Cabeza de Vaca this was the beginning of four years of prolonged hardship. He suffered bad treatment from the Indians and from nature. "I had to get out roots to eat from under the water and from among the reeds where they grew in the ground and from this my fingers were so worn that they bled if a straw touched them." Hunger and cold beset him. At times he was no more than a slave.

To free himself from dependence upon his

Indian masters, Cabeza gradually set himself up as a trader, traveling among the often hostile Indians to exchange the shells, sea beans, and goods from the coast for the skins, ocher, and flints of the interior.

Each year Cabeza returned to Malhado to try to persuade Lope de Oviedo, the only Spaniard left on the island, to depart with him in search of Christians. Not until 1533 did Oviedo agree. He could not swim, but Cabeza managed to get him to the mainland and across the first four rivers. Down the coast they came upon other Indians who told them that farther on there were three men, two of whom looked like the Spaniards. These Indians also knew of the fate of other members of the expedition. All had died of cold or hunger or had been killed by the natives—for sport or in obedience to omens which had come to the Indians in dreams. While Cabeza and Oviedo waited for the other Spaniards, the natives abused them, holding drawn arrows against their chests and telling them that they were going to be killed. Oviedo's courage failed him. He departed for Malhado, and disappeared from history.

Two days later Alonso de Castillo and Andres Dorantes, and Estevanico, his slave, arrived with their Indian masters, and the four men rejoiced much at finding one another alive. For more than a year the three Spaniards and the black man lived as slaves of the Indians, who fed mainly on roots, but also ate spiders, worms, caterpillars, lizards, and snakes. Though Cabeza describes them as thieves, liars, and drunkards, they were at the same time "a merry people, considering the hunger they suffer." The women did the camp labor.

"Cattle came here," Cabeza says, "and I have seen them three times, and partaken of them. It seems to me that they are the size of those of Spain. They have small horns . . . and very long hair, flocky, like a merino's. Some are tawny, others black, and it seems to me that they have better and fatter meat than those of Spain. From the smaller ones the Indians make blankets to cover themselves, and from the larger ones they make shoes and shields. They come from the north over the land to the coast, spreading out over all the country more than 400 leagues, and along

A 16th-century French sketch of a buffalo based on accounts by explorers like Cabeza de Vaca.

their route and the valleys by which they come, the people who live nearby descend upon them and live off them." Thus, the first description of the American buffalo.

In the summer of 1533, the Spaniards and the slave were brought by the Indians to the prickly-pear fields (most likely south of San Antonio). Before the prisoners could escape, the Indians fell to quarreling and took up their lodges and left. The four Christians (for Estevanico was a Christian) were denied by this dispute an opportunity to escape, and were separated once again, to spend another year in captivity.

After the passage of these hard months, the Indians reassembled to gorge on tunas, the purple fruit that grows from the edges of a flat-leaved, spiny cactus. Here the four men learned they were indeed the last survivors of the Narvaez expedition.

Finally, as the moon grew full in September, 1534, the Spaniards and the slave slipped away from their masters. Shortly they came upon another tribe, the Avavares, who received them well.

Winter was not far off, and the natives told the Spaniards that the country ahead was poor in game and abandoned by the Indians in the cold months. The travelers decided to remain where they were. They stayed with the Avavares for eight months.

In the late spring or early summer of 1535, the wanderers started again on their quest for Mexico. Now the pattern of their lives changed. They had acquired a reputation as medicine men, and as they moved from tribe to tribe, they were met with rejoicing. Perhaps at this stage of their journey they crossed the lower Rio Grande and entered Mexico. They were still lost, and still hundreds of miles from the nearest Spanish settlements to the south at Panuco. But their march took on the character of a triumphal procession. At each village the Indians brought the sick to be cured, and then escorted the travelers to the next settlement.

When the wanderers came in sight of the mountains of northeastern Mexico, they made what seems a strange decision. They turned from the coastal plain and headed inland, away from the direct route to the Spanish settlements. Cabeza gives the reason for this change—fear of the evil disposition of the coastal Indians, in contrast to the good treatment received from the inland tribes. He also hints that these indomitable men swung away to the west and north in search of the riches and fabled cities that had eluded them since they had sailed from Spain eight years earlier.

Perhaps also they took pleasure in their prosperity and power. Laden with gifts, which they distributed as fast as they were received, and exercising such authority over the awed and superstitious Indians that none dared to take a drink of water without permission from the strangers, the four wandered on.

Along river valleys and across mountain ridges they went west and northwest through northern Mexico. The land was rugged and dry, except in the verdant valleys. In this country the travelers were given corn flour. And Cabeza worked a true cure (of his other "cures," he was always careful to point out that the Indians *believed* they had been cured). He operated on an Indian who had been shot by an arrow, removed the arrowhead from deep in the man's chest, and with a deer bone as a needle sewed up the wound.

Now they had roast quail and venison to eat. On they went, crossing "a great river," probably the Rio Grande again, near the Big Bend. Then, after journeying 250 miles through dry, rough country, they again forded "a very large river," having come back once more to the Rio Grande, farther north. Here they saw houses rather than huts, and the Indians gave them corn, pumpkins, and beans.

The years had hardened the four men physically and confirmed them in their faith: "We used to walk all day without eating until night, and we ate so little that the Indians were astonished to see it. . . . We passed through a great many peoples of diverse tongues; with all of them Our Lord God favored us."

Week after week they walked westward from the Rio Grande, across northwestern Mexico, over the passes of the Sierra Madre, down the western mountain valleys toward the coast, into a land of relative plenty. The Indians brought the Spaniards corals from the Gulf of California and turquoises from the pueblo country of Arizona and New Mexico. The wanderers made their way south, threading the valleys between the mountains and the ocean. Now, news about other Christians became frequent, but it was bad news, at least for the Indians. A Spanish slaving expedition had left the fertile countryside deserted, the villages burned, and the remaining inhabitants hidden in the mountains. Still the Indians who had come with the four travelers continued to journey on, assured by Cabeza of his protection. One morning near the Petatlan River (now the Sinaloa), Cabeza "came upon Christians on horseback, who received a great shock to see me, so strangely dressed and accompanied by Indians. . . . I told them to bring me to where their captain was . . . and I asked him to give me a certificate of the year and the month and the day on which I had arrived there and the manner in which I came, and thus it was done."

By the Sinaloa River, not far from the Pacific Ocean and about 100 miles north of the border settlement of San Miguel, the odyssey of Cabeza, Dorantes, Castillo, and Estevanico ended. The Indians accompanying the "gods" did not wish to abandon them until they had been conveyed into the safekeeping of other Indians, nor did these Indians wish to lose their protectors, for fear of the other white men.

Cabeza relates that the slave-hunting Christians "took offense at this and made their interpreter tell the Indians that we were people of no account, and that they were the lords of that land, who had to be obeyed and served. . . . The Indians said that the Christians lied, because we came from where the sun rises, and they whence it sets; that we healed the sick, while they killed the sound; that we came naked and barefooted, while they came clothed and on horses and with lances; and that we were not covetous of anything, while the others had no aim but to rob everything."

Cabeza finally persuaded the Indians to return to their homes and fields, and he thanked them and dismissed them in peace. With an escort, the four travelers started on their way to Mexico City. But their efforts to protect the natives from the slave hunters had endangered their own lives. Only the arrival of a well-disposed higher official saved Cabeza and the others from possible death at the hands of their own countrymen.

From the border settlement of San Miguel they pushed on 300 miles to Compostela, then another 500 miles to Mexico City. There they were joyfully received and honored by the viceroy, Mendoza, and by the conqueror, Cortez. The harsh imprint of their journey was still upon them, for Cabeza tells that it was some time before he could stand the touch of clothes upon his body, or sleep anywhere but upon the ground.

Cabeza reached Spain the following summer, but by 1540 he was again in the New World, now as governor of Paraguay. Political difficulties led to his recall and imprisonment; he returned to Spain and obscurity until his death, perhaps in the 1550s.

Castillo and Dorantes settled in Mexico.

It was the black Christian from North Africa, Estevanico, who died like the conquistador he was. Incited by the rumors of civilizations and treasures in the unknown lands to the north of the regions crossed by Cabeza and his companions, Viceroy Mendoza sent out an expedition led by Fray Marcos de Niza. Its guide was Estevanico. He was killed in 1539 by Indians in the pueblo country of New Mexico, having blazed the trail that would be followed, a year later, by Coronado.

Thomas F. McGann was professor of Latin American history, University of Texas. He wrote Argentina, the United States and the Inter-American System, 1880–1914; *and was co-editor of* The New World Looks at Its History.

Tales of de Vaca's journey prompted Spain to send Coronado to find the Seven Cities of Cibola. In this Frederic Remington painting, he is crossing the plains of Kansas in 1541.

Volume I
ENCYCLOPEDIC SECTION

The two-page reference guide below lists the entries by categories. The entries in this section supplement the subject matter covered in the text of this volume. A **cross-reference** (*see*) means that a separate entry appears elsewhere in this section. However, certain important persons and events mentioned here have individual entries in the Encyclopedic Section of another volume. Consult the Index in Volume 18.

COLONIAL GOVERNORS

John Carver (Plymouth)
Hernando Cortez (Mexico)
Sir Ferdinando Gorges (Maine)
Sir Richard Grenville (Roanoke)
Sir Ralph Lane (Roanoke)
Antonio de Mendoza (Mexico)

Peter Minuit (New Netherland)
Juan de Oñate (New Mexico)
Francisco Pizarro (Peru)
Juan Ponce de Leon (Florida)
John Smith (Jamestown)
Petrus Stuyvesant (New Netherland)
Cristobal Vaca de Castro (Peru)

COLONIAL PROMOTERS

Richard Clyfton
Jean Baptiste Colbert
Dutch West India Company
Sir John Popham

Sir Walter Raleigh
Cardinal Richelieu
Sir Edwin Sandys
Kiliaen Van Rensselaer
Virginia Company of London

COLONIES AND COLONISTS

Virginia Dare
Darien
Fort Christina
Fort Orange
Greenland Colony
Hispaniola
Jamestown

Manhattan Island
New Amsterdam
New Sweden
Pilgrims
Puritans
Roanoke Island
John Rolfe

EXPLORERS

Diego de Almagro (Spain)
Hernando de Alvarado (Spain)
Vasco Nuñez de Balboa (Spain)
Jean de Brebeuf (France)
Etienne Brulé (France)
Alvar Nuñez Cabeza de Vaca (Spain)
John Cabot (England)

Sebastian Cabot (England)
Pedro Cabral (Portugal)
Jacques Cartier (France)
Thomas Cavendish (England)
Samuel de Champlain (France)
Christopher Columbus (Spain)
Francisco Vasquez de Coronado (Spain)

Hernando Cortez (Spain)
Vasco da Gama (Portugal)
John Davis (England)
Hernando De Soto (Spain)
Bartholomeu Diaz (Portugal)
Sir Francis Drake (England)
Eric the Red (Scandinavia)
Leif Erikson (Scandinavia)
Sir Martin Frobisher (England)
Sir Humphrey Gilbert (England)
Sir Ferdinando Gorges (England)
Sir John Hawkins (England)
Bjarni Herjulfson (Scandinavia)

Henry Hudson (England, Holland)
Thorfinn Karlsefni (Scandinavia)
Ferdinand Magellan (Spain)
Panfilo de Narvaez (Spain)
Jean Nicolet (France)
Alonso de Ojeda (Spain)
Francisco Pizarro (Spain)
Marco Polo (Venice)
Juan Ponce de Leon (Spain)
Sir Walter Raleigh (England)
Jean Ribaut (France)
Giovanni da Verrazano (France)
Amerigo Vespucci (Portugal, Spain)
Vikings (Scandinavia)

INDIANS

Atahualpa
Aztecs
Huayna Capac
Incas
Machu Picchu
Massasoit

Montezuma II
Mound Builders
Pocahontas
Powhatan
Temple of the Sun
Tenochtitlán

MYTHS AND LEGENDS

Fusang
Kensington Stone
Newport Tower
Norse sagas

Plymouth Rock
Quetzalcoatl
Quivira
Saint Brendan
Seven Cities of Cibola

RELIGION

Jean de Brebeuf
Charles I
Church of England

Marcos de Niza
Pilgrims
Puritans
Separatists

ROYAL SPONSORS OF EXPLORATION

Charles I (Spain)
Elizabeth I (England)
Ferdinand of Aragon
Henry IV (France)

Henry VIII (England)
Henry the Navigator (Portugal)
Isabella of Castile
James I (England)

SHIPS, MAPS, AND NAVIGATION

astrolabe
caravels
Juan de la Cosa
galleons
Line of Demarcation

Mayflower
navigation
Spanish Armada
Paolo Toscanelli
Vinland map
Martin Waldseemüller

SOCIAL AND ECONOMIC INSTITUTIONS

Gregorian calendar
Introduction of horses
maravedi

Mayflower Compact
mercantilism
repartimiento
tobacco

A

ALMAGRO, Diego de (1475?–1538). Almagro played a leading role in the conquest of the **Incas** (*see*), one of history's most dramatic and brutal episodes. His parents were peasants from New Castile. In Panama he joined with **Pizarro** (*see*) to explore and conquer Peru in 1524. Because of various supply problems and the resistance of the Incas, this was not accomplished until 1533. Almagro later undertook his own unsuccessful expedition (1535–1537) to Chile. He returned to Peru to find Pizarro determined to rule the Inca Empire without his participation. Almagro seized Cuzco, the capital city, and marched his army toward Lima to confront Pizarro. He was defeated by Pizarro's forces at the Battle of Las Salinas in April, 1538. Almagro was taken prisoner, put on trial, and executed. However, the bitter rivalry of the two conquistadors was not over. In 1541, a group of Spaniards led by Almagro's half-caste son Diego, who was known as Almagro the Lad (1520–1542), murdered Pizarro. (*See* **Vaca de Castro.**)

ALVARADO, Hernando de (dates unknown). As captain of artillery for **Coronado** (*see*), Alvarado was credited with saving his commander's life during a battle with some rebellious Indians. Later, he was sent to scout the area east of New Mexico and reached the Rio Grande, which he named *Rio de Nuestra Señora* (River of Our Lady). He returned with news of fertile lands and Indian pueblos and brought along an Indian captive who told stories of a kingdom to the northeast (present-day Kansas) called **Quivira** (*see*).

ASTROLABE. This important instrument of **navigation** (*see*) had its origins in the Near East, perhaps in Chaldea, long before the birth of Christ. It was introduced into Europe by the Arabs about A.D. 700. The name comes from the Greek words meaning "star" and "to take." Astronomy, however, was only one of the astrolabe's uses. It was used to measure the height of mountains. Columbus used it to calculate latitude by figuring the angle of the sun above the horizon at noon. The astrolabe was replaced in 1731 by Hadley's quadrant, which was the forerunner of the modern sextant.

ATAHUALPA (1500?–1533). Atahualpa was the last great leader of the **Incas** (*see*). The expedition of **Pizarro** (*see*) reached southern Peru in 1532 soon after the conclusion of a civil war between Atahualpa and Huascar (1495?–1533), the sons of the dead ruler **Huayna Capac** (*see*). The victorious Atahualpa, now undisputed Lord Inca, met the Spaniards at Cajamarca. Tricked into an ambush, he was taken prisoner and about 2,000 of his followers were slain. Atahualpa struck a bargain with Pizarro to purchase his freedom for a ransom that has been estimated at about 13,000 pounds in gold and twice that amount in silver. Pizarro took the gold and silver but did not keep his promise to release the Inca. Instead, Atahualpa was put on trial and convicted of the false charge of inciting his people to revolt. In exchange for his consent to being baptized, Atahualpa was spared the humiliation of being burned at the stake and was instead strangled to death in 1533.

AZTECS. The great Aztec civilization—conquered by the Spaniards in Mexico—was founded on the ruins of the Toltec Empire. The Aztecs, a barbarous and ambitious tribe, invaded central Mex-

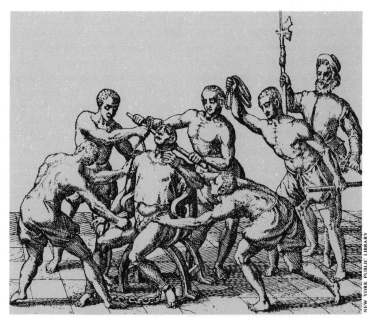

Atahualpa asked to be garroted rather than burned alive at the stake.

ico during the 13th century. The purpose of the invasion was not to conquer territory. Instead, the Aztecs needed thousands of human sacrifices to satisfy the demands of their warlike gods, the chief of which was Huitzilopochtli. Having conquered the local natives, the Aztecs founded their capital city of **Tenochtitlán** (*see*) on the present site of Mexico City. They then concentrated their efforts on the development of perhaps the finest Indian civilization in the New World. They spoke a language called Nahuatl and wrote with glyphs (pictures). A system of tribunals was set up to administer justice, and an efficient communications network enabled the Aztecs to rule their various provinces well. Their artists and craftsmen, particularly their sculptors, produced a brilliant variety of cultural objects. Aztec society was divided into four parts. The nobility owned large private estates. A second group was allowed to share property collectively. The last two groups were the *mayeques* (serfs), who worked for the nobility, and the slaves, who had been captured from other tribes. The Aztec government was composed of civil servants and priests. These priests performed countless human sacrifices, and cannibalism was sometimes practiced as part of the ritual. When **Cortez** (*see*) invaded the Aztec Empire in 1519, he was welcomed peacefully because the Aztecs thought he was **Quetzalcoatl** (*see*), one of their gods. The Spaniards were received at the capital by **Montezuma II** (*see*), leader of the Aztec nation. But friendly relations between the natives and the Spanish did not last. When the Indians began to revolt, Cortez was forced to fight the Aztecs in battle in 1521. The courage of the Indian warriors

and their incredible acceptance of death made a strong impression on the Spaniards. This fatalistic attitude was part of the Aztec religion and is explained in the following Aztec hymn:

We only came to sleep
We only came to dream
It is not true, no, it is not
*   true*
That we came to live on the
*   earth.*
We are changed into the grass
*   of springtime*
Our hearts will grow green again
And they will open their petals
But our body is like a rose tree:
It puts forth flowers and then
*   withers.*

B

BALBOA, Vasco Nuñez de (1475–1517). Balboa was the first European to see the Pacific. He had come to the New World about 1500 to find gold but failed. He then turned to farming at the Spanish outpost of **Hispaniola** (*see*) but did so poorly that he could not pay his debts. To escape his creditors, Balboa stowed away in 1510 on a ship carrying supplies to the colony established by **Alonso de Ojeda** (*see*) at San Sebastian, Colombia. The captain, Martin Fernandez de Enciso (1470?–1528), permitted Balboa to remain on the ship after he was discovered. Balboa took over command of the relief force when San Sebastian was found in ruins and Enciso was unable to cope with the situation. Enciso was put aboard a ship and sent home to Spain. Balboa then sailed southward in search of gold. Stopping on the northern coast of the Isthmus of Panama, he founded the settlement of **Darien** (*see*) in 1510. As its governor, Balboa treated

Vasco Nuñez de Balboa

the natives with a kindness unusual for a conquistador. One friendly chief, the Cacique Comogre, told him about the Inca Empire, which he said was situated beyond the isthmus and a great "South Sea." There, the Indian said, "The people eat and drink from golden dishes and . . . gold is as cheap to them as iron is to you." Recruiting 90 men and hundreds of Indians, Balboa immediately set off across the 45-mile isthmus, expecting to reach the other side in six days. Instead, the crossing took three weeks, and the number of Spaniards was reduced to 69 by disease, snakes, swarms of ants, and hostile natives. On September 25, 1513, Balboa saw the great expanse of the Pacific from a hilltop. He waded into the ocean four days later and claimed "all the sea and all the lands bordering upon it" for the Spanish crown. Meanwhile, Enciso had returned to Spain and turned **Ferdinand** (*see*) against Balboa. Balboa was subsequently relieved of his governorship and replaced by Pedrarias Davila (1440?–1531). Governor Davila, angry at Balboa for writing the king about his cruelty to the Indians, arrested him. Balboa was tried for treason and publicly beheaded at Acla, a town near Darien, on an autumn day in 1517.

BREBEUF, Jean de (1593–1649). Brebeuf, the son of a Normandy landowner, led a Jesuit mission to New France (Canada) in 1625. Its aim was to seek converts in the New World. Brebeuf's base of operations was Quebec, but he lived among the Hurons for three years, teaching Christianity and learning the Indian language. His missionary work was interrupted when the British captured Quebec in 1629. Brebeuf and his fellow Jesuits, along with the French governor, **Champlain** (*see*), were transported to England. In 1634, two years after a treaty was concluded, Brebeuf rejoined the Hurons. Five years later, a smallpox epidemic killed more than half the tribe. At about the same time, the Iroquois launched a series of major attacks on the weakened Huron settlements. During a raid in 1649, Brebeuf and another priest were captured. Brebeuf was tortured mercilessly for four hours before being stabbed to death. Throughout this torture he cried out his faith in Jesus Christ. The Huron mission was abandoned, the tribe itself dissolved, and its members dispersed. Brebeuf was elevated to sainthood by the Roman Catholic Church in 1930.

BRENDAN, Saint (A.D. 484–577). According to a medieval legend, this Irish monk crossed the Atlantic in a kayak and arrived at a "Land of the Gods" that some historians maintain was America. The voyage allegedly took place between A.D. 565 and 573. He was accompanied by 40 other monks. They first discovered Iceland and then supposedly continued sailing for 40 days and nights before reaching North America. The possibility that Brendan and the other monks settled in North America is mentioned in a Viking saga. While **Thorfinn Karlsefni** (*see*) was in the vicinity of the New England coast, according to this saga, the Indians told him of a land "opposite their own where people lived who wore white clothes . . . and carried poles and went with flags."

BRULÉ, Etienne (1592?–1633). Brulé was one of the most successful of the numerous young Frenchmen sent out by **Champlain** (*see*) to explore the Canadian wilderness. While living with Indians near Lake Huron in 1612, he became probably the first European to see one of the Great Lakes. He visited Lakes Erie and Superior as well and is sometimes credited with discovering Lake Ontario in 1615. Brulé explored as far south as Chesapeake Bay on missions for Champlain. He defected to the British about the time that Quebec was captured from the French in 1629. Brulé later returned to live with the Hurons, but they turned against him and, in 1633, killed and ate him.

C

CABEZA DE VACA, Alvar Nuñez (1490?–1557?). A Spanish explorer, Cabeza de Vaca was one of the four survivors of the expedition led by **Narvaez** (*see*) to Florida. Their perilous seven-year journey (*pp. 83–88*) took them across the Southwest and down the west coast of Mexico. When they finally arrived in Mexico City in 1535, their tales of enormous herds of "hunchbacked cows" (buffalo) and exaggerations about the wealth of the Pueblo Indians were circulated throughout the Spanish colony. These stories prompted the expeditions of **Coronado** and **De Soto** (*see both*). Cabeza de Vaca returned to Spain in 1537 and published *Los Naufragios* (The Shipwrecked Men), an account of his experiences in the New World. In 1540, he was appointed governor of the Rio de la Plata region of Paraguay. It took him about two years to reach Paraguay. He was not a popular governor, and in 1544 he was arrested by the colonists. They charged him with improper conduct of office and sent him back to Spain. He was found guilty and banished to Africa. However, **Charles I** (*see*) later pardoned Cabeza de Vaca, gave him a pension, and appointed him a judge of the supreme court of Seville.

John Cabot

CABOT, John (1450–1498). Born in Genoa as Giovanni Caboto, Cabot later became a citizen of Venice and gained much experience in navigation on trading voyages to the eastern Mediterranean. Obsessed with the idea of finding a sea passage to Asia, Cabot moved to England, where, eight years before Columbus made his historic discovery, he tried to enlist financial support for a similar exploration. When Cabot's expedition finally sailed in 1497, it went with the blessing of the king, Henry VII (1457–1509). His ship, the *Mathew*, carried a crew of 18 that included his son **Sebastian Cabot** (*see*). On June 24, after 52 days at sea, Cabot landed at Cape Breton Island, Canada, and unfurled England's royal banner for the first time in the New World. Cabot believed he had reached Asia and was disappointed that he did not find silks and precious stones. On his second voyage in 1498, he explored the eastern coast of Greenland and the northeastern coast of the United States. He died shortly after his return to England, and it was not until many years later, during the reign of **Elizabeth I** (*see*), that the English began seriously to exploit the resources and opportunities of the lands he had claimed in their name.

CABOT, Sebastian (1476?–1557). Only 20 when he made his first voyage to the New World with his father, **John Cabot** (*see*), Sebastian went on to become a noted cartographer and explorer. He commanded a Venetian expedition (1525–1530) to search for Cathay (China) but was diverted by tales of vast riches in South America, and spent four years exploring the Rio de la Plata region. Upon his return, he was punished for not completing his mission and sent into exile in Africa. Eventually, he made his way to England, where in service to the crown, he founded the Merchant

Adventurers of London in 1551. This company was responsible for establishing trade with Russia.

CABRAL, Pedro (1460?–1526). Cabral was commissioned in 1500 by King Emanuel of Portugal (1469–1521) to establish commercial relations with India and to set up trading posts along the Malabar coast. He sailed from Lisbon on March 9 of that year, with 13 ships. Sailing west of the course he had been told to follow, he was carried by the equatorial currents to the coast of Brazil. He took possession of the land in the name of Portugal and detached a ship to Lisbon with the news. He resumed his voyage eastward to India but lost four ships—including the vessel carrying **Diaz** (*see*)—in a violent storm off the Cape of Good Hope. After establishing a trading post at Calicut, Cabral returned to Lisbon in 1501. The personnel he left behind in Calicut were massacred by the populace. Their deaths were later avenged by **da Gama** (*see*).

A typical caravel

CARAVELS. These small, swift-sailing vessels were used extensively by the Spanish and Portuguese explorers in the 15th and

16th centuries (*see* **Columbus, da Gama,** and **Diaz**). They carried from two to four masts and were usually rigged with lateen sails. These triangular sails enabled the caravels to steer better into the wind and thus made them easier to maneuver than the heavier, clumsier **galleons** (*see*). The caravels were built with their decks close to the water. Although they often had a high bow and a high stern, these ships proved hard to keep afloat in stormy seas.

CARTIER, Jacques (1491–1557). The St. Lawrence River was discovered and named by this French navigator during his second expedition to the New World (1536–1537). His first expedition was undertaken two years earlier in the hope of discovering the long-sought Northwest Passage to the Orient. Cartier at that time befriended a band of Huron-Iroquois Indians in the Gulf of St. Lawrence. When he returned to the gulf on his second trip, he encountered another Huron tribe. Its members told him that he had entered *Canada*—the Huron word for "village." Cartier explored the St. Lawrence as far west as the Indian settlement at Hochelaga (now Montreal) before turning back. He returned to Canada in 1541 and prepared to search for a legendary country that the Hurons told him contained vast riches. The Indians insisted that he could reach this land by following the Ottawa River to the north. The mission proved fruitless. Cartier returned to France. There he remained a technical adviser to subsequent expeditions until his death on September 1, 1557.

CARVER, John (1576?–1621). The first governor of the Plymouth Colony, Carver was a wealthy

In 1587, Cavendish sacked a Spanish settlement at Puna Island (Ecuador).

trader in London before religious persecution drove him out of England. Immigrating to Holland in 1609, he joined the Pilgrims (*see* **Separatists**). Carver contributed considerable sums to their finances and became one of their leaders. He organized the group of Pilgrims who sailed directly from England to North America and was responsible for chartering the *Mayflower* (*see*). He sailed aboard the *Mayflower* in 1620 and, while the ship was at sea, was elected governor of Plymouth Colony, under the terms of the **Mayflower Compact** (*see*) of November 11, 1620. During the first difficult winter ashore, Carver helped to nurse the sick. He was reelected governor the following March but died, possibly as a result of sunstroke, on April 5, 1621, while working in the colony's fields.

CASTRO, Vaca de. *See* **Vaca de Castro.**

CAVENDISH, Thomas (1555?–1592). Cavendish was an extravagant Elizabethan courtier who went to sea to make money. After a preliminary voyage to North America in 1585 with **Sir Richard Grenville** (*see*), Cavendish decided to imitate **Sir Francis Drake** (*see*) and sail around the world, plundering foreign ships and colonies. He left from Plymouth, England, in July, 1586, with three ships and returned two years and 50 days later. Two of his ships were lost. While circumnavigating the globe, he sailed down the east coast of South America and discovered Port Desire in Patagonia, which he named for his ship, the *Desire*. During the voyage, Cavendish looted 19 vessels, including a Spanish treasure ship. However, he fell into debt in England and

decided to make another voyage. He set out with five ships in 1591. This expedition failed completely. Cavendish died on the voyage home in the summer of 1592 and was buried at sea.

CHAMPLAIN, Samuel de (1567?–1635). This French mapmaker and adventurer spent 32 years (1603–1635) exploring and promoting eastern Canada, particularly the Great Lakes and the St. Lawrence River system. Because of these efforts, Champlain is frequently called the Father of New France. He first saw the New World as the commander of a ship that was part of a Spanish fleet headed for New Spain. During the voyage (1599–1601), Champlain sketched numerous native plants and animals. His drawings greatly impressed **Henry IV** (*see*) of France, who urged Champlain to join a small fur-trading expedition in 1603 to the lands discovered by **Cartier** (*see*) in North America. Champlain spent the next five years exploring the coast of New

England as far south as Plymouth Harbor. He received royal permission to establish a fortified settlement at Quebec in 1608. The following spring, Champlain accompanied a Huron Indian war party into what is now upper New York State. On the shores of the lake that now bears his name, Champlain and his party met a large Iroquois force. When the Frenchmen fired their guns, the Iroquois fled in terror, permitting Champlain to map the lake in peace. The assassination of Henry IV in 1610 forced Champlain to return to Paris the next year for a new charter for his colony. Back in Quebec, Champlain again joined forces with the Hurons and attacked an Iroquois encampment. Wounded during the battle, Champlain spent the winter (1615–1616) recovering in a Huron village. When he was well enough to travel, he sailed again for Paris, where his maps and commentary on the Great Lakes region were published. Through his efforts, a trading colony called the Hundred

Samuel de Champlain

Associates (*see* **Richelieu**) was formed in 1627 to establish more Canadian colonies. War broke out between England and France shortly after Champlain once again returned to Quebec. The colony was captured in 1629, and Champlain and other French officials and missionaries were transported to England. After the war was settled, Champlain returned to Quebec in 1633. A year later he organized the expedition on which **Nicolet** (*see*) became the first white man to reach the shores of Lake Michigan and Lake Superior. On Christmas Day, 1635, he died.

CHARLES I (1500–1558). Charles was king of Spain at a time when Spanish acquisitions in the New World reached their peak. He was the grandson and heir of **Ferdinand** (*see*) and Isabella. During Charles I's reign (1516–1556), Mexico was conquered by **Cortez** (*see*), Peru fell to **Pizarro** (*see*), and various other expeditions in Central and South America were undertaken. In governing these new lands, Charles tried to protect the natives from slavery and extermination, though to avoid bloodshed he was often forced to withdraw certain reforms in the

face of protests by the Spanish colonists (*see* **Mendoza**). He succeeded to the throne of the Holy Roman Empire in 1520 and ruled it as Charles V. The Protestant Reformation took place while he was emperor. In 1521, Charles, a devout Catholic, convened the Diet of Worms, which condemned Martin Luther (1483–1546) as a heretic. He also supported the Council of Trent (1545–1563), which started the Counter Reformation. This reform of the Catholic Church was intended to protect Catholic tradition from the changes sought by the Protestants. During the last two years of his rule, Charles gradually turned over the control of Naples, the Netherlands, and Spain to his son, Philip II (1527–1598). In 1556, he gave up his last title, and his brother, Ferdinand I (1503–1564), became the Holy Roman Emperor. Charles then retired to live quietly near a monastery in Spain, where he died on September 21, 1558.

CHARLES V, Holy Roman Emperor. *See* **Charles I.**

CHURCH OF ENGLAND. The issues that led to the creation of the Church of England were deeply involved with royal authority. **Henry VIII** (*see*) had centralized his political power by eliminating Rome's control of the English branch of the Catholic Church. The reign (1547–1553) of his young son, Edward VI (1537–1553), strengthened the position of the English church. But Edward's successor and half sister, Mary Tudor (1516–1558), demanded a return to Roman Catholicism. During her brief reign (1553–1558), hundreds of Protestants were burned as heretics, resulting in a rise in anti-Catholic sentiment and an unfortunate

nickname for the queen, Bloody Mary. While **Elizabeth I** (*see*) reversed her half sister's policy and strengthened the state church, dissension was growing between High Church supporters (Anglicans) and those who wanted the church purified (Puritans). Elizabeth's successor, **James I** (*see*), was not tolerant of religious dissent. At the Hampton Court Conference in 1604, James proclaimed that he would not tolerate any deviation from the official positions of the Church of England. This policy was emphasized by James' son, Charles I (1600–1649), during whose reign (1625–1649) the **Puritans** and **Separatists** (*see both*) were forced to conform or emigrate. As a result, tens of thousands left England between 1618 and 1642 for the West Indies and North America.

CIBOLA, Seven Cities of. The fabled cities were first reported by **Cabeza de Vaca** (*see*), one of the survivors of the ill-fated Narvaez expedition (*see pp. 83–88*). His tale of fabulous wealth among the Pueblos was probably a combination of Spanish and Indian tradition. An old Spanish legend told about seven Portuguese bishops who, fleeing the invading Moors, had founded seven cities of great wealth on an island in the Atlantic. There was also the counterfeit tale an Indian slave related about the seven cities rich in gold and silver that were situated in what is today the southwestern United States. A Franciscan friar, **Marcos de Niza** (*see*), was sent north in 1539 by the Spanish viceroy of Mexico, **Mendoza** (*see*), to scout for these cities, and he delivered a glowing report. Observing the Zuñi pueblos of New Mexico from a cautious distance, Niza mistook the adobe walls gleaming in the sunshine for gold. The military conquest of these poverty-stricken villages a year later by **Coronado** (*see*) led in turn to a two-year continuation of the expedition in search of still another mythical city, **Quivira** (*see*).

CLYFTON, Richard (1553–1616). Clyfton was rector of the Separatist congregation in Scrooby, England (*see pp. 54–55*). This center of religious dissension was one of the strongholds of the Separatist movement (*see* **Separatists**). Clyfton and many of his followers fled to Holland in 1607 and 1608 to escape religious persecution. He is best remembered for his influence on the men who led the **Pilgrims** (*see*) to the New World. Clyfton died in Amsterdam four years before the *Mayflower* (*see*) set sail for Plymouth.

COLBERT, Jean Baptiste (1619–1683). Colbert, who was the French finance minister during the reign of Louis XIV (1643–1715), set up the French East India and West India trading companies in 1664. In doing so, he hoped to make them as successful as the Dutch and English trading monopolies already operating in the Orient and the Americas. However, Colbert wanted to control completely the operations of both companies, and he insisted on rigid money regulations. His inflexibility, together with the reluctance of French financiers to back his plan, brought about the failure of the trade ventures in 1682. After Colbert's death, the East India Company was revived and flourished until the end of the Seven Years War (1756–1763).

COLUMBUS, Christopher (1451–1506). The discovery of the Americas by Columbus opened the way for the colonization of the Western Hemisphere by European nations and changed the course of history. The son of a weaver of modest means, Columbus is generally believed to have been born in Genoa, Italy, where he was called Cristoforo Colombo. Speculation exists that he was, among other things, of French or Jewish origin. He studied geography and astronomy at Pavia University and may have corresponded with the famous Florentine geographer, **Toscanelli** (*see*). He married the daughter of a Portuguese captain, earned his living as a sailor and mapmaker, and worked on plans for his "enterprise of the Indies." Columbus was convinced that the wealthy markets of the Orient could be reached not only by sailing east, as the Portuguese were trying to do, but also by sailing west across the Atlantic. No one in Europe then knew that the western route was blocked by a "New World" stretching almost from pole to pole. Needing funds for his venture, Columbus appealed about 1483 to John II of Portugal (1455–1495) but was rejected. The king was more interested in the African route projected by **Henry the Navigator** (*see*), and he also considered Columbus "a big talker and boastful," who demanded too many rewards for himself. Columbus subsequently submitted his plans to **Ferdinand** (*see*) and Isabella of Spain. Six years passed before they finally agreed to finance his expedition. Columbus sailed from Spain on August 3, 1492, with the *Santa Maria*, the *Pinta*, and the *Niña*. After a delay of four weeks for repairs in the Canary Islands, the ships continued west with favorable winds. By mid-September, however, they were becalmed in seaweed in the Sargasso Sea. The crews became frightened, and Columbus spent the next three weeks preventing mutiny. On October 12, a small island in the Bahamas was sighted. Sailing south, Columbus discovered other islands, including Cuba and **Hispaniola** (*see*), all of which he claimed for Spain. On Christmas Day, the *Santa Maria* went aground off Hispaniola. Columbus salvaged her timbers, built a fort, and put 44 men ashore to establish the first Spanish colony in the New World. Anxious to announce his discoveries, Columbus returned to Spain aboard the *Niña*. He was greeted with great enthusiasm, and his discovery (which he believed was part of Asia) became known throughout Europe. A new fleet of 17 ships and 1,500 men was immediately prepared and set sail in September, 1493, with Columbus in command. It reached Hispaniola eight weeks later to find the fort destroyed and his colonists dispersed by hostile "Indians." Columbus founded a new colony on the island, but owing to trouble with the natives and internal dissension, it did not thrive. Complaints against his administration were sent to Spain, and Columbus returned in 1496 to answer the charges against him. Following his acquittal, Columbus set out on a third voyage in 1498, during which he discovered Trinidad and the coast of Venezuela. Further complaints against him led to his arrest by Francisco de Bobadilla (?–1502), and he was brought back to Spain in chains. Again exonerated but stripped of his rank and honors, Columbus left on his final voyage in 1502, still seeking a water route that would lead westward to Asia. During this voyage, he discovered Honduras and visited the Isthmus of Panama. He returned to Spain in 1504 and died at Valladolid on May 20 or 21, 1506, still convinced he had reached the outskirts of Asia.

CORONADO, Francisco Vasquez de (1510–1554). Arriving in Mexico in 1535 in the retinue of **Mendoza** (*see*), first viceroy of New Spain, Coronado married a wealthy and influential woman. He became governor of the province of New Galicia in 1538. When the Spaniards heard the exciting, though erroneous, reports of incredible wealth to the north in **Cibola** (*see*), Mendoza appointed Coronado the commander of what was described by a contemporary as "the finest expedition ever launched." The expedition (1540–1542) covered more than 3,000 miles and was one of history's most remarkable explorations, though it was a financial disappointment from beginning to end. Cibola turned out to be a poverty-stricken settlement of Zuñi pueblos. Coronado and his small army then headed farther north, encouraged by the false reports of a Plains Indian named Turk, who insisted that there existed a kingdom called **Quivira** (*see*) that would more than fulfill the Spaniards' craving for gold. The expedition crossed through the present-day Texas Panhandle and Oklahoma in 1541. Quivira turned out to be a desolate area, sparsely settled by Wichita Indians, probably in what is today central Kansas. The major achievements of Coronado's expedition—the first credible account of the Zuñi pueblos, the discovery of the Grand Canyon, the increased geographic knowledge of the area, and the large addition to Spain's territorial claims in the New World—were ignored by his colleagues. They considered his long journey a failure because he returned to

Mexico empty-handed. The explorer himself paid a heavy price for his part in the expedition. His fortune was depleted and his health broken. For several years, Coronado was under investigation for his official conduct as governor of New Galicia. He was accused of maltreating the Indians and accepting bribes. Although at first he was found guilty, removed from office, and fined, he was exonerated in 1551 and awarded a pension for his services.

CORTEZ, Hernando (1485–1547). The conqueror of treasure-laden Mexico was born in Spain of noble though poverty-stricken parents. He studied law briefly but gave it up for a life of adventure. In 1504, he became a planter in Santo Domingo and seven years later helped to conquer Cuba. When reports were received of the fabulous treasure in Mexico, he was chosen by the Spanish governor of Cuba to command an expedition against the **Aztecs** (*see*) in 1518. Cortez landed in Mexico the following year and subdued the Tabascans, a tribe under the control of the Aztecs. Cortez soon received emissaries from the Aztec emperor, **Montezuma II** (*see*), who sent precious gifts but no invitation to visit the capital city, **Tenochtitlán** (*see*). Instead of reporting all this to the governor of Cuba, Cortez sent one of his ships directly to **Charles I** (*see*) in Spain. He destroyed his remaining ships and began his march inland toward the Aztec capital with 400 soldiers and 17 horses. Along the way, he gathered allies among the Indians who hated Montezuma. But when the Spaniards reached Tenochtitlán, they were treated as honored guests. The Aztecs were afraid that Cortez was either an important Indian god, **Quet-**

zalcoatl (*see*), or one of this deity's priests. Montezuma publicly turned over his vast treasuries of gold and silver to Cortez, who accepted in the name of Charles I. Meanwhile, the jealous governor of Cuba had sent another army in 1520 to subdue Cortez. Leaving 200 of his men in the capital, Cortez marched back to the coast and defeated this second army, which was commanded by **Narvaez** (*see*). However, the sight of the Spaniards fighting among themselves confused the Aztecs, who soon revolted. Returning to Tenochtitlán, Cortez and his men were forced to retreat from the city. The following year, the Spanish attacked and destroyed the island city. Most of the treasure given Cortez was lost. Although Montezuma's nephew claimed that the missing gold had been thrown into the lake, Spanish divers found nothing. The disappointed conquistadors enslaved the Aztecs and forced them to work in gold mines. Cortez remained in Mexico as the military governor. But his

The Aztec capital Cortez captured is represented on his coat of arms.

reign was marred by native revolts and investigations from Spain. He finally was replaced in 1535 by a viceroy, **Antonio de Mendoza** (*see*), sent from Spain. Cortez was given a title by the king and decorated, but he never again controlled Mexico. He died near Seville on December 2, 1547.

COSA, Juan de la (1460?–1510). Cosa was a pilot on the first voyage of **Columbus** (*see*) to the New World in 1492. He also accompanied Columbus on his second voyage in 1493. Six years later he joined **Alonso de Ojeda** (*see*) in exploring the northern coast of South America. In 1500, Cosa drew the first map of the known world (*see pp. 24–25*). This map cast doubt on whether the newly discovered lands were part of Asia, as Columbus mistakenly assumed. Cosa was killed by Indians in 1510 while on another expedition with Ojeda.

DA GAMA, Vasco (1469?–1524). An experienced soldier and mariner, da Gama was chosen about 1496 by King Emanuel of Portugal (1469–1521) to explore a sea route from western Europe to Africa. The feasibility of such a voyage had already been established in 1488 by **Bartholomeu Diaz** (*see*). Da Gama left Lisbon in 1497 in command of a flotilla of four ships specially built for the mission. He rounded the Cape of Good Hope without loss, sailed up the east coast of Africa, and finally arrived at Calicut in southwest India during May, 1498. He tried to establish a trading post, but the Moslem merchants there feared this new competition and incited the Hindu populace against the Portuguese. Da Gama, con-

Vasco da Gama

vinced of the great value of trade with India, returned to Lisbon in 1499 and was honored by the king. A second expedition was immediately dispatched to India under **Pedro Cabral** (*see*), who also attempted to set up a trading post. After his departure, Cabral's men in Calicut were slaughtered. Da Gama returned in 1502 with 10 heavily armed ships. He bombarded the town and treated its inhabitants with brutality. Sailing south to the town of Cochin, he attacked all the shipping he encountered along the way. Da Gama succeeded in obtaining favorable trading terms from the local rulers and returned to Lisbon in 1503 with valuable cargoes. Now one of the richest men in Portugal, he retired. Twenty-one years later he was recalled by Portugal's John III (1502–1557) and appointed viceroy of India, but he took sick and died at Cochin shortly afterward.

DARE, Virginia (1587–?). On August 18, 1587, Ellinor White Dare, the daughter of the governor of the colony at **Roanoke Island** (*see*), gave birth to the first English child born in the New World. The infant girl was christened Virginia, which was the name given the area in honor of the "virgin queen," **Elizabeth I** (*see*). The baby disappeared with the other members of that ill-fated colony a few years later. The mystery has never been solved.

DARIEN. Spaniards led by **Balboa** (*see*) established this colony on the northern shore of the Isthmus of Panama in 1510. The entire isthmus was also called Darien, which is what the 19th-century poet John Keats meant when he referred to Darien in his sonnet, "On First Looking into Chapman's Homer" (1816). Wrongly identifying the Pacific Ocean's discoverer as **Cortez** (*see*) rather than Balboa, Keats wrote that Cortez

> . . . *star'd at the Pacific—and all*
> *his men*
> *Look'd at each other with a wild*
> *surmise—*
> *Silent, upon a peak in Darien.*

DAVIS, John (1550?–1605). One of the leading navigators who served **Elizabeth I** (*see*), Davis participated in at least eight major voyages of exploration. He tried three times in the 1580s to find a northwest passage to China. In the course of his searches, he explored the coasts of Greenland. On one voyage, his ship ran into a "furious overfall" of water at the mouth of Hudson Strait. Davis decided not to explore the waterway, thus missing the opportunity to discover Hudson Bay. In 1588, Davis helped **Drake** (*see*) and others turn back the **Span-**

ish **Armada** (*see*). Three years later he left England on a fourth voyage to the American continent. When the leader of the expedition, **Thomas Cavendish** (*see*), turned back, Davis went on alone. His route carried him south to the Strait of Magellan at the southern tip of South America. Davis spent the next three years (1593–1596) in England, where he published *The Seaman's Secrets*, a practical manual for navigators. After a trip to the Azores (1596–1597) with **Raleigh** (*see*), Davis sailed for the Orient (1598–1600) with an expedition outfitted by the Dutch East India Company. He made another trip there (1601–1603) in the employ of the British East India Company. On his third voyage to Asia, Davis was killed by Japanese pirates. His last name is sometimes spelled Davys.

DE OJEDA, Alonso. *See* **Ojeda.**

DE SOTO, Hernando (1500?–1542). Although the mouth of the Mississippi River may have been sighted by early explorers, De Soto is generally credited with discovering in 1541 the river called the Father of the Waters. As a young man, he had accumulated a fortune in Central America and Peru, where in 1532 he helped **Pizarro** (*see*) conquer the Incas. Returning to Spain, he became one of its richest citizens and may even have lent money to **Charles I** (*see*). That monarch in 1537 appointed De Soto governor of Cuba and *adelantado* (civil and military chief) of the lands of Florida. After fitting out at his own expense an expedition that included 600 men, 10 ships, arms, horses, cattle, pigs, and hounds for terrifying the Indians, De Soto sailed from Spain and anchored off the east coast of Florida in 1539. His

party then made its way across the southeastern portion of North America in search of treasure. There was continued warfare with the natives, much of it apparently instigated by De Soto, whom another Spaniard described as "very fond of the sport of killing the Indians." About 30 miles from the present site of Memphis, Tennessee, the band of adventurers came in 1541 to a great river, which was so wide, one of them later wrote, "A man standing on the opposite shore could not have been recognized as a man." De Soto's men built barges, crossed the river, and continued as far west as Texas. Wearied after three years of fruitless wandering, the expedition returned to the Mississippi River, where De Soto fell ill and died on May 21, 1542. His followers weighted De Soto's body with sand and sank it in the river at night, so that the Indians would not find out that the Spanish leader had died. Only 311 men managed to survive the 700-mile trip down the Mississippi to the Gulf of Mexico.

Hernando De Soto

Bartholomeu Diaz

DIAZ, Bartholomeu (1450?–1500). This Portuguese explorer was commissioned in 1486 by King John II of Portugal (1455–1495) to extend the exploration of the West African coast started by **Henry the Navigator** (*see*) in his search for a new trade route to India and the Far East. Diaz left Lisbon in 1487 with two ships and proceeded down the African coast. He sailed past Cape Cross, the southernmost point previously reached by Portuguese explorers. Driven by strong following winds, Diaz found himself in stormy seas beyond the sight of land. He rode out the storms and turned east to regain the coast. Failing to sight land after several days, he then headed north and reached the south coast of Africa on February 3, 1488. His sailors were anxious to return home, but Diaz insisted on following the coastline eastward, convinced that the route around Africa to the Indies had at last been found. During the return voyage, Diaz discovered Africa's cape peninsula, the southern tip of which he named Cape of Storms. This name was later changed to Cape of Good Hope by King John. Diaz apparently received little or no reward for this great service to his country. He was given minor positions in subsequent expeditions and was eventually lost at sea in a gale off the cape he had so aptly named.

DRAKE, Sir Francis (1545?–1596). Born in Devonshire, England, of a devout Protestant family, Drake was regarded by Englishmen as "the greatest of privateers" and "the greatest of Royal Admirals." He is especially celebrated for his part in the defeat of the **Spanish Armada** (*see*) in 1588. As a privateer, he harried Spanish towns and shipping in the West Indies. He sailed through the Strait of Magellan in 1578 in the *Golden Hind,* and with less than 100 men, plundered the Spanish settlements up the coasts of Chile and Peru. He claimed the California coast for **Elizabeth I** (*see*) and called it New Albion. He then completed his voyage around the world in less than three years. For these exploits he was knighted by the queen.

DUTCH WEST INDIA COMPANY. In 1621, a group of Dutch merchants received an exclusive franchise from their government and formed the Dutch West India Company. Its purpose was to establish fortified colonies and engage in trade along the coasts of the Americas and Africa. The company's American holdings included the Hudson River Valley colonies of **New Amsterdam** and **Fort Orange** (*see both*) and several islands in the Caribbean. The venture was a commercial failure in spite of the fact that it had been patterned on the highly successful Dutch East India Company, which operated in the Pacific. The company lost its possessions in North America to the British in 1664 but continued to operate in the West Indies, South America, and Africa for another decade. A new Dutch West India Company was set up in 1675. It carried on a slave trade in the same areas until the decline of the slave market in the late 18th century. This second company was dissolved in 1791.

E

ELIZABETH I (1533–1603). Elizabeth was the daughter of Anne Boleyn (1507–1536) and **Henry VIII** (*see*). She succeeded her half sister, Mary Tudor (1516–1558), to the throne in 1558 at a time when England was confronted with religious dissension (*see* **Church of England**), economic difficulties, and troubled foreign relations. She encouraged exploration in the New World as an extension of her foreign policy against Spain, whose power was eventually broken by the defeat in 1588 of the **Spanish Armada** (*see*). The commercial growth of England during her reign was paralleled by scientific and cultural achievements of the highest order, so that today historians refer to the entire period as the Elizabethan Age. Among the best-known explorers encouraged by the queen were **Sir Francis Drake, Sir John Hawkins, Sir Humphrey Gilbert,** and **Sir Martin Frobisher** (*see all*). By 1603, when the "virgin queen" died, England was on her way to becoming the world's greatest sea power.

ERIC THE RED (dates unknown). The father of **Leif Erikson** (*see*), Eric the Red started the westward migration of the **Vikings**

Honored by California's Indians, Drake claimed their land for England.

(*see*). Banished from Iceland in A.D. 982 for killing a man, Eric crossed the Denmark Strait and reached Greenland, a land that had previously been sighted but never explored. He found a fertile strip on the southwest coast and decided to establish a colony there (*see* **Greenland Colony**). To lure settlers away from Iceland, Eric did not mention the island's subarctic climate, but rather, as an Icelandic saga goes, called it "Greenland, because, he said, men would be the more readily persuaded thither if the land had a good name." Fourteen boatloads of colonists arrived in Greenland about 986. They managed to eke out a living. When Leif Erikson sought to convert the Greenlanders to Christianity about 1002, he "was well received by every man" except his father, who objected to such missionary work and later separated from his wife after her conversion.

ERIKSON, Leif (dates unknown). The son of **Eric the Red** (*see*), Leif probably reached the shores of North America by accident about the year A.D. 1000. According to an Icelandic saga, Leif was sent by the king of Norway in 999 "to proclaim Christianity" to his native Greenland. However, his ship was thrown off course by storms and "came upon lands of which Leif had previously no knowledge." Leif's first landfall was at a flat rocky coast that he named Helluland (thought to be Labrador). Traveling southward, he came upon a low-lying wooded land with great expanses of white sand. Although he was probably still off the coast of Labrador, he named this Markland. Still farther down the coast (estimates by historians place Leif as far south as Chesapeake Bay), he stopped and

wintered in a region with a mild climate that he named Vinland because of the grapes he found growing there. Leif returned to Greenland the following spring with a cargo of lumber and vines. He subsequently devoted himself to converting his countrymen to Christianity. The next scouting expedition to Vinland was made by Leif's brother Thorvald in 1004. He wintered in Leif's old camp, and while exploring the area the next year, was killed by Indians. In 1008, another brother, Thorstein, undertook to retrieve Thorvald's body, but his ship lost its way in a storm. After reaching the western shore of Greenland, Thorstein became ill and died. Leif's last name is sometimes spelled Ericson, Ericsson, Eriksen, or Eriksson.

F

FERDINAND of Aragon (1452–1516) and **ISABELLA of Castile** (1451–1504). Although the marriage of these monarchs in 1469 occurred before they had succeeded to their respective thrones, it eventually unified Spain. Until then, Spain was made up of four independent kingdoms: Aragon, Castile, Granada, and Navarre. Isabella was proclaimed queen of Castile in 1474 and shared the throne with Ferdinand, although the crown was hers alone and she was the actual ruler. On Ferdinand's succession to the throne of Aragon in 1479, the two kingdoms were united. The royal couple conquered Granada in 1492, after a 10-year war, thus ending the Moorish occupation of Spain. Ferdinand's conquest of Navarre in 1512 completed the unification of the nation. During their reign, the infamous Inquisition was es-

Ferdinand and Isabella accept a book from a monk in this 1502 woodcut.

tablished to enforce religious obedience and conformity. One of the first steps it took was to expel the Jews in 1492. This was followed by the expulsion of the Moors in 1502. Isabella encouraged **Columbus** (*see*) to seek a new trade route to Asia, a venture that resulted in the well-known formation of a Spanish empire in the New World and the vast enrichment of Spain.

FORT CHRISTINA. *See* **New Sweden.**

FORT ORANGE. This fur-trading outpost was erected in 1624 by the Dutch families sent to colonize the upper Hudson River Valley region. The fort was situated near the site where **Henry Hudson** (*see*) had once anchored the *Half Moon* during his exploration in 1609 of the river that bears his name. The prospering colony surrendered in 1664 to the British, who renamed it Albany. (*See* **Van Rensselaer.**)

FROBISHER, Sir Martin (1535?–1594). This Elizabethan sailor was determined to discover a sea passage to China and the East Indies. After 15 years of trying to raise the necessary funds, he was given command in 1576 of three small ships and 35 men. One of the ships sank in a storm off Scotland and another turned back, but Frobisher sailed on. He reached the Labrador coast after a seven-week voyage. Finding his progress to the north blocked by ice, he decided to explore what is now called Frobisher Bay, which he mistook for a passage to Asia. After five of his men were captured by the Indians, he returned to England with some mysterious "black earth" rumored to be gold ore. Encouraged by this report, **Elizabeth I** (*see*) sent him on two more voyages to Frobisher Bay. But the ore he shipped back to England proved worthless. Frobisher was more successful in his later career as a naval commander. He served as vice admiral (1585–1586) under **Drake** (*see*) in the West Indies

Sir Martin Frobisher

and was knighted two years later for his part in defeating the **Spanish Armada** (*see*).

FUSANG. The "wonderful Land of Fusang"—possibly near Acapulco, Mexico—was allegedly visited and described in the latter half of the fifth century A.D. by a Buddhist missionary from China named Hwui Shan. Fusang, which means "super" or "colossal," had long existed in Chinese mythology as an earthly paradise situated somewhere across the Pacific. In Hwui Shan's account, this legendary land lay 20,000 li (more than 6,500 miles) east of the Kamchatka Peninsula in Siberia. Hwui Shan supposedly crossed the Pacific to the Aleutian Islands and Alaska. He then sailed down the west coast of North America. Arriving in Mexico, Hwui Shan wrote, "That region has many Fusang trees and these give it its name. . . . The people of the country eat [its sprouts]. . . . They spin thread from the bark and make coarse cloth. . . . The wood is used to build houses and they use Fusang bark to make paper." This wondrous growth may have been the *maguey* (century) plant. Archeologists say the Indians of Mexico used it in the various ways that Hwui Shan described. Often reaching a height of 30 feet, the plants could have easily been mistaken for trees. During his 40-year stay in Fusang (458?–498?), Hwui Shan may have made a number of religious conversions. Historians of pre-Columbian civilizations in Mexico have found traces of Buddhism in the Mayan religion. Hwui Shan probably embellished his observations, but it is possible that he did reach the Pacific coast nearly 500 years before **Leif Erikson** (*see*) sailed to Vinland on the Atlantic coast.

G

GALLEONS. These slow but stately vessels carried the treasures of the New World back to Spain. They were also used as troopships, men-of-war, and freighters in the 16th century. They had three or four masts, the foremast and mainmast being square-rigged and the mizzenmast, or aftermast, carrying triangular lateen sails similar to those used on the **caravels** (*see*). Galleons had high superstructures called castles at the bow and at the stern. These ships ranged in size from about 400 to 1,000 tons.

GILBERT, Sir Humphrey (1539?–1583). A half brother of **Sir Walter Raleigh** (*see*), Gilbert was an early advocate of English exploration to locate a northwest passage to Cathay (China) and India. Two years after his famous book on this subject, *Discourse,* was published in 1576, he received a charter from **Elizabeth I** (*see*) to explore and colonize all "heathen lands not actually possessed of any Christian prince or people" in the New World. Gilbert conducted two expeditions in search of a water route to Asia. On the second trip in 1583, he explored the northern coast of Newfoundland. Sailing back to England, Gilbert was last seen by the crew of another ship, seated at the stern with a book in his hand. "We are as near to heaven by sea as by land," he called out. That night the ocean "devoured and swallowed up" his vessel.

GORGES, Sir Ferdinando (1566?–1647). An early advocate of English colonization in North America, Gorges is credited with being the founder of Maine. He was born at Long Ashton, Somersetshire, and was trained as both a sailor and a soldier. He was captured by a ship of the **Spanish Armada** (*see*) in 1588 but was soon freed. In 1591, he was knighted for his services to France at the siege of Rouen. Five years later, Gorges was appointed military leader of Plymouth, England. He joined **Sir John Popham** (*see*) in 1607 in sponsoring the Popham Colony on the Kennebec River in present-day Maine. After it failed, Gorges continued to sponsor fishing, trading, and exploring expeditions in the colonies. In 1620, he helped secure from **James I** (*see*) a new charter that reorganized the Virginia Company of Plymouth (*see* **Virginia Company of London**) as the Council for New England. Although Gorges failed in his attempts to become the governor general of New England, he was awarded the royal charter of Maine in 1639. This province was gradually absorbed (1652–1658) by Massachusetts, whose Puritan government was openly hostile to Gorges, a strong advocate of the **Church of England** (*see*). Gorges died in England in 1647.

GREENLAND COLONY. This Norse settlement that **Eric the Red** (*see*) founded along the southwestern shore of Greenland about A.D. 986 was a trading post for more than four centuries. About 16 years after the colony was started, **Leif Erikson** (*see*) converted the Norse inhabitants to Christianity. Eventually, 16 churches and a stone cathedral were built in the colony. The climate of the island—actually almost 85% of it is a permanent ice cap—was milder than it is today, but survival was a constant struggle for the settlers. There was very little land for crops and only a

small strip for grazing. Most colonists were forced to make a living by fishing or by hunting whales, reindeer, seals, and bears. Iron was found, but there was not enough fuel for large-scale smelting operations. Norway took possession of Greenland in 1261 and sent one ship annually to the outpost until the early 15th century. At the time of Columbus, Pope Alexander VI (1431–1503) observed that no word had been received from the colony for about 80 years. The settlers might possibly have been killed by Eskimos. More likely, they died from malnutrition. Over the years, Greenland's climate had grown progressively colder, and there was increasingly less vegetation to feed the colonists or their cattle.

GREGORIAN CALENDAR. In 1582, Pope Gregory XIII (1502–1585) ordered the use of a "reformed" calendar to replace the Julian (or Old Style) calendar. The Old Style, established in 45 B.C. by Julius Caesar, had accumulated a number of errors over the centuries until the calendar was no longer in step with the actual season. The Gregorian (or New Style) calendar was adopted almost immediately by the Roman Catholic countries of Europe. Britain and her colonies, however, did not switch to the Gregorian calendar until 1752. This has led to discrepancies in historical writing because English manuscripts written prior to 1752 are dated in the Old Style. To correct this, 10 days must be added to the given date. That correction has been made in these volumes. All dates are in the New Style.

GRENVILLE, Sir Richard (1541?–1591). An agent of his cousin, **Sir Walter Raleigh** (*see*), Grenville

was co-commander with **Sir Ralph Lane** (*see*) of the first attempt to colonize **Roanoke Island** (*see*) in 1585. Grenville sailed back to England for additional supplies, but when he returned to the colony in 1586, he found it deserted. The men he left at Roanoke to garrison the colony until more settlers could be sent had apparently been massacred by the Indians before a new expedition could be dispatched. Grenville later served with distinction in naval combat with the Spaniards. His death in 1591 followed a heroic battle against overwhelming Spanish forces off the Azores.

H

HAWKINS, Sir John (1532–1595). Along with **Drake** (*see*), Hawkins gained a reputation during the 1560s as a privateer who, in the service of England, plundered the Spanish colonies in the West Indies and Latin America. He also robbed Portuguese slave ships and then sold the slaves to Spanish colonists. For his part in the defeat in 1588 of the **Spanish Armada**, he was knighted by **Elizabeth I** (*see both*). His coat of arms, approved by the queen, bore the image of a chained black slave.

HENRY IV (1553–1610). Known also as both Henry of Navarre and Henry the Great, this French monarch tried to revive the prosperity of his nation by developing agriculture, industry, and foreign trade and by attempting to colonize New France (Canada). He was raised as a Protestant in Catholic France, and supported the Huguenots (Protestants) in their wars with the French Catholics (1562–1598). He became king when Henry III (1551–1589) was

Henry IV

assassinated. Henry IV formally converted to Catholicism in 1593 to quiet his political opponents. However, he decreed in the Edict of Nantes in 1598 that there would be religious and civil toleration for all French Protestants. In 1603, he granted a charter to **Champlain** (*see*) to explore the North American continent. This charter resulted in the founding of Quebec in 1608. Henry was assassinated by a religious fanatic on May 14, 1610.

HENRY VIII (1491–1547). Henry, England's second Tudor king, ascended to the throne upon the death of his father, Henry VII (1457–1509). In fulfillment of his dying father's request, Henry married Catherine of Aragon (1485–1536), daughter of **Ferdinand** (*see*) and Isabella of Spain and the widow of his older brother, Prince Arthur (?–1502). Five children were born to the couple, but only one daughter, Mary (1516–1558), survived. Desperate for a legitimate male heir, Henry sent his lord chancellor to Rome to secure the permission of Pope Clement VII (1478–1534) for a divorce. The pope, under pressure from

Catherine's powerful Spanish relatives, refused. Henry went ahead and married Anne Boleyn (1507–1536) in 1533. This marriage was declared valid by Thomas Cranmer (1489–1556), whom Henry had appointed the archbishop of Canterbury. Parliament now began enacting a series of laws that severed England's legal and financial ties to the Vatican. This process culminated—17 years after the start of the Protestant Reformation—in the Act of Supremacy in 1534, which declared Henry the supreme head of the **Church of England** (*see*). Rome's valuable property in England was confiscated the next year and divided between the king and his nobles. Anne Boleyn, the queen, who had given birth in 1533 to one child, **Elizabeth I** (*see*), was accused of adultery and executed in 1536, a fate shared by another of Henry's next four wives.

HENRY THE NAVIGATOR (1394–1460). John I of Portugal (1357–1433) appointed his third son, Prince Henry, the governor of the province of Algarve, but the prince is remembered best for his contributions to naval science that launched Portugal as a pioneer in nautical exploration. At Sagres, a port in southern Portugal, he founded a school of astronomy and navigation that attracted mariners from all over Europe and helped to standardize the knowledge of geography. The improvements made at his school on the compass were invaluable to open-sea navigation. Soon, armed **caravels** (*see*)—a type of small fast ship developed at Sagres— were sailing west to the offshore islands and along the Atlantic coast of Africa, probing for a passage to the East. Prince Henry died before a "passage" was

found, but his inspiration resulted in the voyages of **Bartholomeu Diaz** (*see*) around the Cape of Good Hope in 1488 and of **Vasco da Gama** (*see*) to India in 1498.

HERJULFSON, Bjarni (dates unknown). This seafaring trader, rather than **Leif Erikson** (*see*), may have actually discovered the New World. According to one of the two Icelandic sagas about voyages made by the **Vikings** (*see*), Bjarni sailed from Iceland in A.D. 986 for Greenland, where he planned to spend the winter. On his way, "The fair wind died out, and north winds arose, and fogs, and they knew not whither they were drifting." Bjarni knew from other Vikings' descriptions what Greenland looked like, so when he sighted an unfamiliar coast he knew it was not the island. Again, spotting land farther north, Bjarni doubted that it was Greenland either, because there were no "great ice-mountains." After drifting past land a third time, Bjarni headed out to sea and finally arrived at the cape of Greenland. Bjarni's three landfalls correspond with Leif's later accounts of the new lands he had sighted.

HISPANIOLA. Hispaniola is the second-largest island in the West Indies. It lies between Cuba, which is the largest, and Puerto Rico. Hispaniola is 407 miles long and 160 miles wide. When **Columbus** (*see*) first discovered the island, it was inhabited by about 2,000,-000 natives, who called the island *Haiti* (mountain country). The Spaniards made the island their base of operations in the Caribbean. They killed off the natives and replaced them with black slaves imported from Africa. The western part of the island was ceded in 1697 to France and, in

1820, became the Republic of Haiti. The eastern two-thirds of the island remained under Spanish rule until occupied by the British in 1793. It acquired independence in 1844 as the Dominican Republic.

HORSES, Introduction of. The chief means of transportation of the Spanish in their exploration and settlement of the Americas, horses were also to provide the Indians of the Southwest with a new mobility in hunting and fighting. In the early 16th century, Spaniards began breeding horses in the West Indies, and soon were supplying the conquistadors with mounts for their mainland expeditions. **Hernando Cortez** (*see*) brought 16 horses and a colt to Mexico in 1519. These animals

With the horse, the Spaniards conquered vast areas of the New World.

played such a major role in the conquest of Mexico that one witness exclaimed, "After God, we owed the victory to the horses." The Spaniards were quite aware of the military advantages of the horse. For 24 years after Cortez landed in Mexico, the invaders were prohibited by royal decree from allowing the Indians to ride horses. When the Spanish established ranches in the Southwest in the early 17th century, the herds multiplied rapidly and many horses strayed. These strays, called *mesteños* (mustangs), were captured by Indians, who quickly learned to ride them. The Indians also stole horses by raiding Spanish settlements. By the middle of the 18th century, horses were being used for hunting buffalo and for combat by Indians in the plains and mountain regions of the West.

HUAYNA CAPAC (1450?–1525?). The reign (1493?–1525?) of Huayna, 11th emperor of the **Incas** (*see*), was a period of turmoil in Peru. Rebellions occurred continually throughout the almost 3,000-mile-long kingdom. In addition, diseases (probably smallpox, measles, and scarlet fever) carried by white explorers and unknown until then to the Indians killed thousands of Incas. Huayna himself fell ill. His decision to divide his empire between his sons Huascar (1495?–1533) and **Atahualpa** (*see*) led to civil war. This conflict further weakened the Incas and paved the way to victory for the invading Spaniards under the command of **Francisco Pizarro** (*see*).

HUDSON, Henry (?–1611). Little is known about this English navigator prior to his departure in 1607 on the first of four attempts to discover a northern sea route

Hudson's Half Moon

to the Orient. Following two inconclusive expeditions under charters from the Muscovy Company (*see p. 66*), a third voyage, financed by the Dutch East India Company, was launched in 1609. Hudson was supposed to sail to the northeast, but his ship, the *Half Moon,* was battered by foul weather off Norway. To calm his rebellious crew, the captain was forced to turn south. After scouting the Chesapeake Bay area, Hudson sailed north along the New Jersey coast up to the tip of Manhattan Island. He then piloted the *Half Moon* up the river that now bears his name, claiming the land on either side—as far north as Albany, New York—for the Dutch government. Hudson's last expedition in 1610 aboard the *Discovery* was marred by dissension and ended tragically. While exploring what he called "a Sea to the Westward" (Hudson Bay), his crew mutinied. Hudson and eight others, including his son John, were set adrift without provisions in the ship's boat on June 23, 1611, and were never heard of again.

I

INCAS. The word *Inca* refers both to the sovereign of the far-flung Peruvian Empire and to an Indian subject of that empire. Tradition has it that the Inca dynasty was founded, possibly in the early 13th century, by Manco Capac, who began to unite the Indians of Peru. By the time of Lord Inca **Atahualpa** (*see*) in the 16th century, the imperial domain incorporated dozens of tribes and stretched from modern Colombia to Argentina and Chile. The Incas' achievements were remarkable. They built structures of superb craftsmanship, such as the **Temple of the Sun** at Cuzco and **Machu Picchu** (*see both*). Although the wheel was unknown to them, their road system, used by relays of swift messengers, rivaled that of the Roman Empire. They developed agricultural terracing and irrigation and discovered quinine for the treatment of illness. Artifacts that have survived Spanish marauders testify to their

Armadillo-shaped Inca oil lamp

artistic genius as potters and metalworkers. The Incas also devised an efficient bureaucracy, a reasonably accurate solar calendar, and despite the lack of a written language, a method of recording history through the use of *quipus* (knotted ropes). The Inca religion was elaborately ceremonial, the chief gods being Viracocha, the Creator, and Inti, the Sun God. Poetry was recited, and dramas were sometimes performed at court festivals. Although precious metals were abundant, the majority of the people lived in relative poverty. Taxes were paid by labor in the Lord Inca's fields and mines. An Inca could not rise above the social status to which he was born. Polygamy was a privilege of

the aristocracy. The language of the Incas, Quechua, is still spoken by many Peruvian Indians. The Inca Empire fell before invading Spaniards (1530–1533), led by **Francisco Pizarro** (*see*).

INDENTURED SERVANTS. Basically, there were three types of indentured servants in the New World. The "free willers" were men and women who signed contracts for three to five years of service in return for passage to America. The second type was made up of convicts and paupers who chose resettlement and seven years of service instead of imprisonment. Finally, there were those who were kidnapped from England and sold as servants to farmers and planters in America for a period of time. Early in the colonial period, a few black people came to America as indentured servants; after completing their service, they became landholders. When the practice of slavery began, however, most of these free blacks were deprived of their rights and were made slaves.

ISABELLA. *See* **Ferdinand of Aragon.**

J

JAMES I (1566–1625). The foreign and domestic policies of England's first Stuart king encouraged the colonization of America. After succeeding to the English throne on the death of **Elizabeth I** (*see*) in 1603, James ended the long conflict with Spain the following year. As a result, English privateers were not permitted to capture Spanish treasure ships anymore. The Spanish, for their part, refrained from interfering with the English settlements and trade in

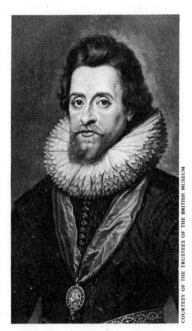

James I

North America. James had hoped that his colony at **Jamestown** (*see*) would provide England with such valuable commodities as silk and wines. But the most profitable item produced by the colony was **tobacco** (*see*), which James had earlier condemned in his famous *Counterblaste to Tobaçço*, published in 1604. In it, he called smoking "vile and stinking" and "dangerous to the Lungs." James was not a popular king. His Scottish accent and slovenly appearance irritated the people, and his insistence on the divine rights of the crown angered the church and the nobility. On matters of religion he was quite firm. He told his subjects either to conform to the **Church of England** (*see*) or to leave the country. His intolerance led to the migrations of the Pilgrims (*see* **Separatists**) and the **Puritans** (*see*). It also led to the Great Rebellion, in which his son, Charles I (1600–1649), was beheaded by the Puritans.

JAMESTOWN. The first enduring English settlement in America was founded in 1607 on a marshy peninsula about 32 miles from the mouth of the James River, named, as was the colony, for **James I** (*see*). Although the site was particularly unsuited for a colony, the settlers began building a fort and huts for shelter. On higher ground, they planted wheat. Almost immediately they were beset by trouble. The Indians attacked them, their houses caught fire, and they suffered from malaria and dysentery from the brackish water. To make matters worse, the colonists were not pioneers but people who considered themselves gentlemen and thought manual labor was degrading. They had come to America to find riches. As **John Smith** (*see*) later wrote, there was "no talke, no hope, nor worke, but dig gold, wash gold, refine gold, load gold." Only the stern discipline imposed by Smith and other leaders kept the settlers from perishing the first winter. During the first year, two more groups of settlers arrived, including the first two women in the colony. The living conditions, however, did not improve. In the colony's third winter (1609–1610), remembered as "the starving time," Jamestown's population shrank from 700 to 60 inhabitants. The dispirited survivors were getting ready to abandon the settlement and return to England when a provision ship arrived. It was not until the commercial cultivation of **tobacco** (*see*) was begun in 1613 that Jamestown started to prosper. North America's first representative assembly, the House of Burgesses, convened there in 1619, the same year that slave labor was introduced. After a fire in 1698, the capital was moved to Williamsburg in 1699.

K

KARLSEFNI, Thorfinn (dates unknown). Drawing inspiration from what **Leif Erikson** (*see*) had reported about Vinland, this Viking trader led a colonizing expedition to the North American mainland early in the 11th century A.D. He embarked with three ships, 160 men, Leif's sister Freydis and other women, and an indeterminate number of cattle. After spending some time on the coast of Labrador, one shipload of disgruntled settlers turned back, but Karlsefni continued southward and finally stopped at a river mouth, possibly situated in New England. He named the encampment Hop. At first the Norsemen traded with the local Indians, bartering red cloth for pelts. Peaceful relations ended abruptly when a colonist's bull charged the Indians, who then fled. Karlsefni's men anticipated their return and built a palisade around their homes. A war party soon arrived in canoes. As described in one of the sagas of the **Vikings** (*see*), the Indians bore a strange weapon consisting of a pole topped with a "great ball-shaped body . . . and this they hurled from the pole up on the land above Karlsefni's followers, and it made a frightful noise, where it fell. Whereat a great fear seized Karlsefni, and all his men, so that they could think of nought but flight and of making their escape." What the weapon was, no one knows. But one person who was not so easily intimidated by it was Freydis. She brandished a sword and routed the Indians. Karlsefni, however, realized that his people would have "a life of constant dread and turmoil by reason of the hostility of the inhabitants of the country." He abandoned this colony and eventually sailed back to Greenland.

This stone is either evidence of early Viking explorers or an historical hoax.

KENSINGTON STONE. If the writing on this 200-pound slab is indeed as old as some believe, the **Vikings** (*see*) traveled as far inland as the Midwest in 1362. The controversial stone, unearthed near Kensington, Minnesota, in 1898, is inscribed in runic letters of the old Scandinavian alphabet. Translated, the runes read, "8 Swedes and 22 Norwegians on an exploration journey from Vinland westward. . . . We were out fishing one day. When we came home we found 10 men red with blood and dead. [They were killed apparently by Indians.] AVM [an invocation to the Virgin Mary] save us from evil. We have 10 men by the sea to look after our ships, 14 days' journey from this island. Year 1362." Language experts and many historians doubt the authenticity of the stone. Some believe that the stone was part of a hoax perpetrated in the 19th century by Scandinavian immigrants who wanted to point with pride to their ancestors.

L

LANE, Sir Ralph (1530?–1603). Lane shared the command of the first settlement of **Roanoke Island** (*see*) in 1585 with **Sir Richard Grenville** (*see*). Physical hardship and Indian hostility forced the colonists to retreat to England after a year. Lane never returned to North America. He later participated in military activities against the Spaniards in the service of **Elizabeth I** (*see*). The remainder of his life was spent on garrison duty in Ireland.

LINE OF DEMARCATION. Originally drawn in 1493 by Pope Alexander VI (1431–1503) at the request of the Spanish throne, the Line of Demarcation was intended to regulate the rights of Spain and Portugal to exploration in the known world. This arbitrary north-south divider was first situated about 300 miles west of the Cape Verde Islands. The pope granted Spain authority in all the lands to the west of the line, and gave Portugal control over lands to the east of it. Portugal protested his decision, and at the Convention of Tordesillas in 1494, the line was moved about 1,000 miles farther west. This still only gave Portugal territorial rights to the eastern bulge of Brazil. In practice, the line did little to prevent conflicts between the two nations.

The pope had no accurate map, as here, for dividing the New World.

M

MACHU PICCHU. Built on an 8,400-foot-high Andean Mountain saddle about 50 miles northwest of Cuzco, Peru, Machu Picchu appears to have been the last stronghold of the **Incas** (*see*) after the Spanish conquest (1530–1533). It is believed to have been built after 1400 and was probably called Vilcapampa by the Incas. Machu Picchu occupies an area about 400 yards by about 350 yards and includes nearly 200 rooms, all skillfully crafted of white granite without the use of mortar. Although surrounded by a strong wall, it may have served originally as a religious retreat rather than a fortress. The reason for its abandonment is unknown. It was rediscovered in 1911 by Hiram Bingham of Yale University.

MAGELLAN, Ferdinand (1480?–1521). This Portuguese-born sailor led an expedition that accomplished what Columbus had dreamed of doing: reaching the Far East by sailing westward from Europe. Magellan had already sailed to India by way of the southern tip of Africa in 1505 in the service of King Emanuel of Portugal (1469–1521) and to the Spice Islands (the Moluccas), in 1511.

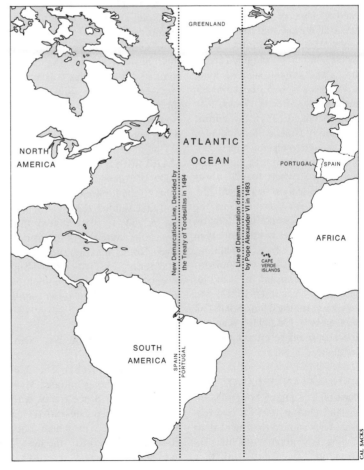

After his return to Portugal, he fell into royal disfavor during a campaign against the Moors in Morocco in 1513. Accused of trading with the enemy, he immigrated to Spain in 1517 and offered his services to **Charles I** (*see*). Magellan persuaded the Spanish king that India and the Spice Islands could be reached by sailing west around the still unexplored tip of South America. With the king's support, he set sail in 1519 with five ships and about 275 men. The first few months were spent exploring the coast of Brazil. After putting down an attempted mutiny, Magellan sailed into the strait that now bears his name, and after 38 days of difficult sailing, entered the ocean that he called the Pacific. One of the ships was wrecked during the passage and another deserted and turned back. As the other three continued across the Pacific without sighting land, provisions and water began to run out. Finally, after 14 weeks, they sighted Guam in the Ladrone (Marianas) Islands. Staying only long enough to replenish their supplies, they sailed on to the Philippine Islands, where Magellan was killed by natives on April 27, 1521. The survivors reached the Spice Islands, where they took on a cargo of cloves worth more than the entire cost of the expedition. Down to one ship, the *Vittoria,* under the command of Juan Sebastian del Cano (?–1526), the survivors returned to Spain on September 6, 1522. They were the first Europeans to circumnavigate the globe.

MANHATTAN ISLAND, Purchase of. The Dutch bought Manhattan Island in 1626 for two reasons. They wanted to cement their trading advantage with the Indians on the island, and they hoped to secure Indian support against the possible claims by the French and the English. The negotiations with the local Canarsee chieftains were conducted by **Peter Minuit** (*see*), the director general of New Netherland. He agreed to pay 60 guilders' worth of trading goods and trinkets. Minuit named the island **New Amsterdam** (*see*). The transaction was, in a sense, a double swindle. The Dutch payment—variously estimated at between $24 and $2,000—was obviously a pittance for an island so rich in game and arable soil. On the other hand, the Canarsee Indians did not have any legal right to sell Manhattan. The northern three fourths of the island was inhabited and "owned" by the Weckquaesgeeks, another Algonquian tribe. The Weckquaesgeeks were understandably upset, and their hostility toward the Dutch resulted in a series of brutal massacres by both sides. By the time the English took control of New Amsterdam in 1664, few Indians were left on the island.

MARAVEDI. Columbus gave 5,000 of these Spanish copper coins to the lookout on the *Pinta* who first sighted the New World (*see p. 11*). It is estimated that these coins were worth about half a cent each, making the reward total about $25. Two hundred and seventy-two maravedis amounted to one piece of eight (later called the peso).

MARCOS DE NIZA. *See* **Niza**.

MASSASOIT (?–1661). The chief of the Wampanoag Indians, Massasoit signed a peace treaty with the Pilgrims (*see* **Separatists**) on March 22, 1621, in which both sides promised not to "doe hurte" to each other. It was agreed that any Pilgrim breaking the peace would be punished by the Indians. Similarly, any Indian who broke the peace would be punished by the Pilgrims. In addition, neither the Indians nor the Pilgrims could carry weapons into each others' territories. Following the treaty, the Indians were frequent visitors to Plymouth. Squanto, a member of the Pawtuxet tribe, taught the Pilgrims how to plant corn. In the fall of 1621, when the corn was harvested, the Pilgrims invited a group of Indians to join them in a feast. This was the first Thanksgiving dinner (*see pp. 80–81*). The treaty between Massasoit and the Pilgrims was never broken. Until his death in 1661, Massasoit remained an ally of the Pilgrims.

The Mayflower *at sea*

MAYFLOWER. The three-masted merchant ship that brought the **Pilgrims** (*see*) to the New World in 1620 was quite small by modern standards. Her 90-foot length was five feet shorter than the beam (width) of the Staten Island Ferry. More than 30 seamen were needed to handle the 180-ton vessel, whose average speed was about 60 miles a day. At the time of her historic voyage to Plymouth under the command of part-owner and master Christopher Jones, the *Mayflower* was being used mainly as a wine-trading ship in the Mediterranean. Before that, her double decks had been packed with everything from fish to timber and tar. She remained with the Pilgrims until they had built lodgings ashore. Then the ship returned to London. Her ultimate fate is unknown. A reproduction of this ship, the *Mayflower II,* was built in England and sailed across the Atlantic in 53 days in 1957. She is now one of the leading tourist attractions at Plymouth.

MAYFLOWER COMPACT. The Mayflower Compact, which declared that the Plymouth Colony would be self-governing, was created out of necessity. After the *Mayflower* (*see*) had anchored in Provincetown Harbor in 1620, arguments began between two groups of Pilgrims over who would rule the new colony. One group of settlers, insisting that "none had the power to command them," threatened to form a separate colony. The rival **Separatists** (*see*), who called themselves the Saints, tried to prevent this by presenting the Mayflower Compact. It proposed the creation of a "civill body politick" that would operate under "just & equall lawes." The document was based on the concept that government exists through the consent of the governed. It was signed aboard the *Mayflower* on November 11, 1620, by 41 adult males. Women, who like servants were considered property, were not allowed to sign. In practice, the Mayflower Compact did not work. The Saints dominated the local government, and Plymouth was more like a theocracy—ruled by ministers of God—than a democracy.

Antonio de Mendoza

MENDOZA, Antonio de (1485?–1552). The first viceroy of New Spain (Mexico), Mendoza was sent there by **Charles I** (*see*) in 1535 to replace **Cortez** (*see*). The Spanish king wanted a loyal and efficient official rather than a power-hungry conquistador in control. Mendoza did much to improve the conditions of the Indians. He established hospitals and schools, he set a maximum on hours for work in the mines, he ordered that both slave and free Indians receive payment for their labor, he protected Indian-owned lands, and he instituted self-government in Indian villages. Although he limited the practice of slavery, Mendoza rejected the attempt by Charles I in 1542 to abolish slavery. Another viceroy in Peru had been killed by the Spanish colonists when he tried to enforce the king's order. Despite two costly expeditions in search of new territorial conquests—one of which was led by **Coronado** (*see*)—New Spain prospered under Mendoza. When Mendoza asked to resign in 1549, he was considered so valuable as

an administrator that Charles I instead appointed him viceroy of Peru, where he died in office.

MERCANTILISM. Mercantilism (*see pp. 44–45*) was an economic theory of the 16th and 17th centuries. It was based on the supply of gold. According to this theory, any nation seeking power needed to have a large surplus of gold. This, in turn, necessitated a great deal of centralized control over colonies by a mother country. Under the mercantile system, colonies were to supply raw materials, such as tobacco, which the mother country could then sell to other nations for gold. In Spain, however, the flow of gold from its Latin-American colonies created inflation. That is, although the supply of gold increased, the amount of goods available for purchase with it remained the same. As a result, the prices of goods increased. The inflation severely weakened Spain and contributed to her decline as a world power. The English subscribed to mercantilism but did not insist upon total control in the New World. Colonies in America were considered self-governing "provinces" of England. Nonetheless, they were economically subordinate and were expected to provide the raw materials for English production. No product could be imported or exported without first having passed through England. This system caused a great deal of resentment in the colonies and was one of the basic causes of the American Revolution.

MINUIT, Peter (1580–1638). As director general of New Netherland (1626–1631), Minuit negotiated the purchase of **Manhattan Island** (*see*) from the Canarsee Indians. Not much is known about his life prior to this time. He was probably of French or Walloon origin, but he was able to speak and write in the Dutch language. Minuit was something of a free-lance adventurer-politician and was often involved in controversy. After he left the employ of the Dutch, he became the governor of **New Sweden** (*see*) in 1638. He died in a hurricane at sea while on a trading mission.

MONTEZUMA II (1480?–1520). Montezuma was the Aztec emperor of Mexico when **Cortez** (*see*) arrived in 1519. Montezuma had reigned for 17 years in the capital city of **Tenochtitlán** (*see*). Before he ascended the throne in 1502, Aztec rulers had been elected. Montezuma changed that. He made himself an absolute monarch and assumed the roles of chief military commander, head of state, and high priest. He also extended the Aztec Empire by conquering more tribes in Mexico. Many of these Indians later gained revenge by joining the Spaniards in battle against the Aztecs. Montezuma was described by one of Cortez's lieutenants as being "about forty years old, of good height and well-proportioned, slender and spare of flesh

Montezuma asked his advisers about dreams of the white man's arrival.

... he had good eyes and showed in his appearance and manner, both tenderness and, when necessary, gravity." Montezuma hesitated to attack Cortez because he mistook him for the Aztec god, **Quetzalcoatl** (*see*). As a result, Montezuma allowed his territory to be occupied by the Spaniards and himself to be made their prisoner. For a while, Cortez used Montezuma to keep the Aztecs under control. But when the Indians revolted and drove the Spanish from Tenochtitlán in 1520, Montezuma was stoned by his rebellious chiefs as he addressed them. Three days later he died of the wounds. His body was dumped into a canal outside the city by the Spanish as they retreated from the Aztec capital.

MOUND BUILDERS. As far back as 3,000 years ago, an Indian group known as the Adena built mounds to bury their dead. The mounds were usually made of logs covered with earth and sometimes rose as high as 70 feet. The Great Serpent Mound, near Locust Grove, Ohio, was named for its winding, curving features. The Adena lived in the Ohio Valley and their mounds are found throughout the Northeast and the lower Great Lakes. About 400 B.C., another Indian group, the Hopewells, constructed similar mounds for their dead. Hopewell mounds are found not only in the Ohio Valley but also in Indiana, Illinois, Iowa, Wisconsin, Michigan, and Missouri. Long after the Hopewells disappeared, tribes of Indians in the Southeast also built mounds, which were shaped like flat-topped pyramids and had temples on top of them. The Indians who built these mounds were known as Temple Mound people. Their civilization, which

A mound-builder temple

covered an area from Oklahoma to Alabama, was in decline by the time that **Columbus** (*see*) discovered the New World. It disappeared soon after the arrival of European settlers. All the mounds contained Indian headdresses, ornaments, pottery, and other artifacts, which help tell much of what America's first inhabitants were like. The shapes of the mounds were so unusual that they were thought at first to be relics of a lost race. Some persons even believed that the mounds were constructed by Egyptians, Vikings, or one of the lost tribes of Israel.

N

NARVAEZ, Panfilo de (1480?–1528). Born a member of the lesser nobility in Spain, Narvaez came to the New World about 1498. He was instrumental in the 1511 conquest of Cuba. Nine years later he was chosen by the governor of Cuba to head the expedition sent to Mexico with orders to capture and imprison the insubordinate **Cortez** (*see*). He lost an eye in the ensuing battle and was himself captured. He was held prisoner for a year by Cortez, who lured most of Narvaez's troops into his own army with promises of wealth through conquest. When released, Narvaez returned to Spain and in 1526 obtained a grant to conquer and govern Florida. His subsequent expedition was a disaster (*see pp. 83–88*). Narvaez drowned in a shipwreck in the Gulf of Mexico in 1528.

NAVIGATION. By modern standards, the few navigational aids available to sailors in the 15th and 16th centuries were crude. **Henry the Navigator** (*see*) had encouraged improvements of the compass, which helped sailors to hold a steady course if the pole star or the sun were obscured. They could tell approximate distance from the equator by measuring the angle of the sun above the horizon at noon with a mariner's **astrolabe** (*see*). This gave them their latitude, but they did not have a reliable way of finding their longitude. They thus were unable to determine their precise position at sea when no landmarks were in sight. The sailors made up for this by careful estimation of the ship's speed and of the length of time spent sailing in a given direction. Clocks had begun to appear in Europe during the 13th century, but they were too inaccurate for use in navigation. Sandglasses were more reliable. Hourglasses, half-hour glasses, and even half-minute glasses were in common use. These smaller glasses were used to calculate the ship's speed through the water. This was done by throwing a "log" into the sea and timing its passage between two points marked on the deck. These methods enabled ships to venture out of sight of land and, eventually, to circumnavigate the earth.

NEW AMSTERDAM. This Dutch settlement on the southern tip of Manhattan Island was founded in 1625 by a small group of Dutch

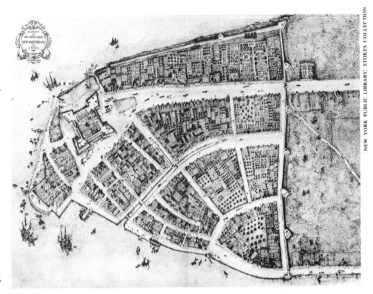

This map depicts New Amsterdam in 1660, when Stuyvesant was governor.

West India Company settlers who were transplanted from nearby Governors Island. The next year Manhattan was purchased from the Canarsee Indians by **Peter Minuit** (*see*). The colonists were joined that same year by Dutch families from **Fort Orange** (*see*), who had been forced to evacuate their Hudson River fur-trading post because of Indian troubles. Fortified, New Amsterdam survived a prolonged Indian war (1637–1645), but when **Petrus Stuyvesant** (*see*) arrived in 1647 to assume control of the colony, he found the settlers disorganized and disorderly and the town's buildings in need of repairs. The settlement prospered under Stuyvesant's rule. New Amsterdam's citizens eventually rebelled against Stuyvesant's dictatorial regime in 1652, but it was five years before they actually received a voice in the government of the colony. Captain Richard Nicolls (1624–1672), who commanded the British squadron that captured New Amsterdam in 1664, changed the

city's name to New York in honor of the Duke of York, later James II (1633–1701).

NEW NETHERLAND. *See* **Stuyvesant, Petrus.**

NEWPORT TOWER. This octagonal, two-story stone structure may confirm descriptions found in the Norse sagas that indicate that the **Vikings** (*see*) landed in

The Newport Tower

E25

New England. Allegedly built between the 11th and 16th centuries, the tower, situated at Newport, Rhode Island, has been variously described as a Viking church, a fortress, or a combination of both. The building does resemble certain medieval structures found in Sweden and parts of Europe. However, most historians believe the tower was a beacon or mill built in colonial times.

NEW SWEDEN (1638-1655). The lone Swedish colony in the New World was established in 1638 by 25 soldiers, who erected Fort Christina on the shores of a small river emptying into the Delaware River. The fort, built on land now within the city limits of Wilmington, Delaware, was the first permanent colony established in the Delaware River Valley. It prospered as additional settlers arrived in 1640, 1641, and 1643. The colony's autocratic governor, Johan Printz (1592-1663), dominated the fur trade in the valley. When the Swedish overwhelmed the Dutch fort at Sandhook, Delaware, in 1653, the Dutch government in Holland was enraged and ordered a retaliation. In 1655, **Petrus Stuyvesant** (*see*), governor of **New Amsterdam** (*see*), led a fleet of seven ships and 300 soldiers south to reclaim the Dutch fort and to capture Fort Christina. He succeeded, and Sweden's brief career as a colonial power ended.

NICOLET, Jean (1598-1642). Nicolet was one of the first Europeans to study the civilization and language of North American Indians. A member of a French exploration party headed by **Samuel de Champlain** (*see*), he observed the culture of many tribes, including the Algonquians, Sioux, Hurons, Illinois, and Potawatomis.

From 1622 to 1631, he lived among the Nipissings and became their official interpreter. Searching for a northwest passage to the Pacific in 1634, Nicolet became the first white man to explore present-day Wisconsin as well as Lakes Michigan and Superior.

NIZA, Marcos de (?-1558). A Franciscan missionary, Niza wrote a misleading account of Indian treasure that inspired the financially disastrous expedition of **Coronado** (*see*) to the mythical **Seven Cities of Cibola** (*see*) from 1540 to 1542. Niza, by then, had already had a remarkable career in the New World. He arrived in Santo Domingo in 1531, and from there he went to Peru. He was reportedly present at the capture and execution of Lord Inca **Atahualpa** (*see*) in 1533. Niza is credited with having founded the Franciscan province of Lima and having written several works describing the natives of Ecuador and Peru. He was made vice commissary general of the Franciscan Order in New Spain (Mexico) in 1539. After reports were brought back by **Cabeza de Vaca** (*see*) of a wealthy civilization in what is now New Mexico, Niza was sent by the viceroy, **Mendoza** (*see*), to investigate. Stopping a safe distance from a Zuñi pueblo, Niza was so impressed by its size that he compared it to Mexico City and suggested that it might contain great wealth. When Coronado discovered the actual poverty of the Pueblos, Niza, who had gone along as guide, was sent back to Mexico City in disgrace. He died there about 18 years later, probably in March, 1558.

NORSEMEN. *See* **Vikings**.

NORSE SAGAS. *See* **Vikings**.

O

OJEDA, Alonso de (1465?-1515). A Spanish conquistador, Ojeda accompanied **Columbus** (*see*) on his second voyage to the New World in 1493. He was captain of one of Columbus' ships and took part in the colonization of **Hispaniola** (*see*). Ojeda subsequently led his own expedition to Venezuela in 1499 and found the fabled pearl fisheries that Columbus had heard about. **Amerigo Vespucci** (*see*) accompanied Ojeda on this voyage as a passenger. In 1508, **Ferdinand** (*see*) appointed Ojeda administrator of the lands on the Caribbean coast of Colombia known as New Andalusia. Leaving Santo Domingo, Hispaniola, Ojeda sailed for Cartagena, Colombia, to establish a colony there and to verify reports of gold. Ojeda's soldiers pillaged Indian villages in the region and tried to capture Indian slaves. The Carib tribe killed half of Ojeda's men with poisoned arrows and wounded Ojeda. Sailing farther down the coast, Ojeda founded San Sebastian in 1509. He left **Francisco Pizarro** (*see*) in charge of the colony and returned to Hispaniola for help. When supply ships reached San Sebastian the next year, Ojeda's men abandoned the colony. Instead, they sailed aboard the relief ships, under the command of **Vasco Nuñez de Balboa** (*see*), south to the Isthmus of Panama, where they founded **Darien** (*see*). Ojeda remained in Santo Domingo until his death.

OÑATE, Juan de (1549?-1624?). Oñate, the first Spanish governor of New Mexico, was the son of the founder of Guadalajara and was married to the granddaughter of **Cortez** (*see*). In 1595, he was awarded a contract for the "exploration, pacification, and conquest of New Mexico." The next year, the expedition set out from New Spain (Mexico). After several delays, it reached the Rio Grande, near present-day El Paso, in April, 1598. Oñate founded a capital at San Juan and began missionary work. He had little trouble with the Indians after he brutally crushed a Pueblo uprising in 1599. Oñate dispatched two costly expeditions—one to Kansas in 1601 in search of the fabled riches of **Quivira** (*see*), the other to the Gulf of California in 1605. Both expeditions failed. Oñate resigned in August, 1607, and notified the viceroy of New Spain that the colony would be abandoned if reinforcements did not arrive by June, 1608. This angered the viceroy, and Oñate was ordered back to Mexico. He was tried and found guilty of misconduct and disobedience in 1614. His punishment was banishment from Mexico City and New Mexico. Oñate may later have obtained a royal pardon, because he is last mentioned in government records as an official visitor in 1624 to mines in Spain.

P

PILGRIMS The term *Pilgrim*—meaning "one who travels in alien lands"—is generally applied to each of the passengers on the *Mayflower* (*see*) in 1620. The designation was applied to them by William Bradford (1590?–1657), the second governor of the Plymouth Colony. Of 102 immigrants to the New World who made the trip, less than half were religious dissenters or **Separatists** (*see*). The rest of the Pilgrims were either tradesmen, shopowners, or servants.

The murder of Pizarro in 1541 is depicted in this Spanish woodcut.

PIZARRO, Francisco (1475?–1541). Conqueror of the vast empire of the **Incas** (*see*), Pizarro was a blend of fierce courage and ruthless ambition. He was the illegitimate son of a Spanish colonel and was a swineherd as a youth. He received no schooling and remained illiterate throughout his life. After news of the discovery of the New World reached Spain, Pizarro accompanied **Alonso de Ojeda** (*see*) on an expedition to the Colombian coast in 1509. In 1513, he was with **Balboa** (*see*) at the discovery of the Pacific. Pizarro became a cattle farmer in Panama. After hearing reports of gold and riches that had been found to the south, he joined **Diego de Almagro** (*see*), a soldier, and Hernando de Luque, a wealthy priest, in a plan to explore and conquer lands on the western coast of South America. They twice reached the shores of present-day Ecuador between 1524 and 1528, but had to turn back both times because of shortages of men and supplies. Pizarro sailed for Spain in 1528, where he won support from **Charles I** (*see*) for

a new expedition. Enlisting the services of several of his brothers, Pizarro returned to Panama. From there he launched a new expedition in 1530 with three ships, 27 horses, and a band of adventurers and ruffians numbering less than 200. After landing on the coast of Peru, he marched to the Inca stronghold of Cajamarca, plundering as he went. Through treachery, Pizarro captured **Atahualpa** (*see*), the Lord Inca, and killed about 2,000 poorly armed Indians on November 16, 1532. The total subjection of the Inca Empire followed. After the conquest of the Indians, fighting broke out among the Spaniards. Pizarro defeated Almagro in battle and had him executed. Pizarro was himself assassinated at Lima on June 26, 1541, by Almagro's half-caste son Diego, known as Almagro the Lad (1520–1542).

PLYMOUTH ROCK. Historians doubt that Plymouth Rock was the original landing place of the **Pilgrims** (*see*) in 1620. The legend of its significance began in the middle of the 18th century. The rock was publicly mentioned at an official celebration of the Pilgrims' landing in 1774. It was broken several times while being moved to different locations in Plymouth. Cemented together, the rock was placed in its present location, a Grecian-style temple, during a ceremony in 1920.

POCAHONTAS (1595?–1617). Matoaka, nicknamed Pocahontas (playful one), was the favorite child of **Powhatan** (*see*), a powerful Indian chieftain. In 1608, when she was only about 13 years old, Pocahontas allegedly persuaded her father to save the life of a captive, **John Smith** (*see*), and thus became immortalized in

American literature. As Captain Smith later described his rescue, the Indians were about to "beate out his brains," but "the Kings

Pocahontas

dearest daughter, when no intreaty could prevaile, got his head in her armes, and laid her owne upon his to save him from death." Pocahontas became a favorite of the Jamestown colonists. She was captured and taken to Jamestown as a hostage in 1613 in retaliation for the Indians' capture of some colonists. During her stay there, Pocahontas was converted to Christianity, baptized, and given the name Rebecca. She married **John Rolfe** (*see*) the following year, and the couple had one son. Accompanying her husband to England in 1616, Pocahontas was received at the court of **James I** (*see*). As she was preparing to return to Virginia in 1617, she was stricken with smallpox and died.

POLO, Marco (1254?–1324). The man who described the wealth and culture of the Orient to Europeans was a Venetian merchant

who toured Asia with his father and uncle. The Polos set out in 1271 on a trading mission to Cathay (China). When they arrived there by a land route three years later, Marco entered the service of Kublai Khan (1216–1294), the Mongol ruler of Cathay. He traveled throughout Cathay as a representative of the khan's imperial council and impressed the khan with his perceptive reports of other lands. After staying in Cathay for 17 years, the Polos decided to return to Europe with a group of Persian envoys. During their voyage home, the Polos visited parts of southern Asia before landing in Persia. They stayed in Persia for several months before returning to Venice about 1295. Three years later, Marco became the commander of a Venetian galley in an unsuccessful war against Genoa. He was captured and put in jail for about a year. He dictated his experiences in Asia to a fellow prisoner, who

Il Milione, BENEDETTO, 1928

Marco Polo

wrote in French, the language of educated men in Europe. The result was *The Book of Marco Polo*. Upon his release, Marco returned to Venice, where he apparently remained until his death. His book describing the fabulous riches of the Orient had an influence on later explorers, including **Christopher Columbus** (*see*).

PONCE DE LEON, Juan (1460?–1521). Ponce de Leon's discovery of Florida in 1513 was a result of his search for a legendary fountain of youth. Born of a noble family in San Servos, Spain, Ponce de Leon is believed to have come to **Hispaniola** with **Columbus** (*see both*) in 1493. He distinguished himself in the conquest of that island and was appointed a provincial governor. The lure of gold led him to subdue Puerto Rico, and he became its governor in 1509. Although now rich and powerful, Ponce de Leon was not content. He heard Indian tales about an island called Bimini that contained a spring, the waters of which were said to make old men young again. Ponce de Leon obtained a commission in 1512 from **Ferdinand** (*see*) of Spain to find and colonize this marvelous isle, reputedly situated in the western Bahamas. He reached the southeastern coast of what is now the United States in 1513. The Spaniards named the new land La Florida, probably because of the beautiful plants they found growing there. Ponce de Leon then headed southward past the Florida Keys to the Tortugas. On his return to Puerto Rico, he was forced to reconquer that island but was only partly successful. In 1515, he led an expedition against the Carib Indians on neighboring Guadeloupe. A second voyage for the purpose of exploring and settling Florida was made in 1521. The Spaniards landed near either Charlotte Harbor or Tampa Bay and were met by fierce Indians. Struck down by an arrow, Ponce de Leon died aboard his flagship a few days later.

POPHAM, Sir John (1531?–1607). With **Sir Ferdinando Gorges** (*see*), Popham sponsored an expedition of the Plymouth Company to "Northern Virginia" (now Maine), where the Popham Colony was founded in 1607 at the mouth of the Kennebec River. Disagreements and a cruel winter soon proved fatal to the fledgling settlement, however, and it was abandoned after less than a year. As lord chief justice of England, Popham had presided at the trial of **Sir Walter Raleigh** (*see*) in 1603. He was in favor of deporting criminals and the unemployed to the New World, both as a punishment and as a source of colonial labor. The Popham Colony, led by his brother George (1550?–1608), was an experiment of this kind. Popham died in England on June 10, 1607, before the Popham Colony was abandoned.

POWHATAN (1550?–1618). Chief Wahunsonacook, whose tribal name was Powhatan, ruled a confederacy of about 30 tribes of Algonquian Indians in the territory of Virginia. Although he was initially hostile to the Jamestown colonists, Powhatan became a friend of **John Smith** (*see*) in 1608 and traded turkeys and corn to the English settlers. In an effort to win Powhatan's allegiance, the English offered to crown him emperor of the Indians. They imported all the official trappings for a coronation, including a gilt crown, pitcher, bowl, and a scarlet cloak. According to Captain

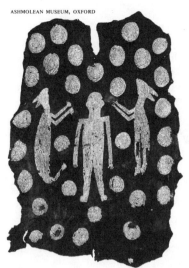

Powhatan gave Smith this deerskin cloak decorated with tiny shells.

Smith, the ceremony confused the new emperor, who, fearing that his life was in danger, had to be forced to his knees:

At last, by leaning hard on his shoulders, he a little stooped and [the English officer] put the Crowne on his head; when, by the warning of a pistoll, the boates were prepared with such a volly of shot, that the king startled up in a horrible feare till he saw all was well.

Powhatan allowed his daughter **Pocahontas** (*see*) to marry an Englishman, **John Rolfe** (*see*) in 1614, thus ensuring peace between the Indian confederation and the colonists. After the chief's death in 1618, hostilities between the Indians and English settlers were renewed.

PURITANS. The Puritans, who settled in the Massachusetts Bay area eight years after the Pilgrims had landed at Plymouth, were less radical religiously than the **Separatists** (*see*). The Puritans wanted to remain within the **Church of England** (*see*) and "purify" it rather than "separate" from it. Another difference between the

groups was their social standing. While the Pilgrims were mostly poor tradesmen and small shopkeepers, the Puritans were members of England's upper middle class. The first group of Puritans to arrive in America in 1628 was led by John Endecott (1589?–1665), who served as governor of a small trading post at Salem (taken from the Hebrew word *shalom*, meaning "peace") until the main body of colonists arrived in 1630, led by John Winthrop (1588–1649).

Q

QUETZALCOATL. This Toltec deity was adopted by the **Aztecs** (*see*) as their god of the morning star. According to legend, Quetzalcoatl and several other gods— all with beards and white faces— had arrived by water from the east. They ruled the Toltecs benevolently for many years before the people revolted and drove them away. As he departed, Quetzalcoatl vowed to return some day and punish the inhabitants of Mexico for their sins. Hence, in 1519, the Aztec emperor, **Montezuma II** (*see*), and his priests mistook **Cortez** (*see*) and the conquistadors for the returning gods and tried unsuccessfully to pacify them with expensive gifts.

QUIVIRA. This mythical kingdom was sought by **Coronado** (*see*) in 1541, after he discovered that there were no riches to be found in the so-called **Seven Cities of Cibola** (*see*). He heard about Quivira from a Plains Indian held captive by the Pueblo Indians. The Indian was called Turk because of the turbanlike headdress he wore. Turk told exciting tales of a kingdom to the north, where the ruler supposedly was lulled to sleep at night by the gentle peals of hundreds of tiny golden bells strung in a tree. Turk claimed to have had a marvelous golden bracelet when he was captured, but the Pueblos refused, even under torture, to confirm his story. Nevertheless, Coronado and his men set out for Quivira with Turk as a guide. Turk led the Spaniards northeast into North America. Finally the expedition arrived at a windswept spot on the plains of Kansas. The Indians called the area Quivira. It was populated by tribes who lived in small groups of huts with roofs of straw. When questioned, Turk admitted that he and his fellow Indians hated the Spaniards and that he had lured them onto the plains so that they would die of cold and hunger. Turk was choked to death on Coronado's orders, and the expedition returned—after a journey of more than 3,000 miles—empty-handed to Mexico in 1542. The legend of Quivira's wealth survived for many years and lured other explorers.

R

RALEIGH, Sir Walter (1552?–1618). Raleigh never set foot on North America, but he twice sponsored unsuccessful colonies in what is now North Carolina, in 1585 and 1587, and sailed himself to South America in 1595 in search of treasure. Raleigh had won the favor of **Elizabeth I** (*see*) by, in part, helping to suppress a rebellion in Ireland in 1580. He was knighted in 1584. Among several royal favors, Raleigh was granted a patent that belonged to his half brother, **Sir Humphrey Gilbert** (*see*). This patent gave him the right to explore, colonize, and

govern territories "not inhabited by Christian people." He sent two ships to explore the Atlantic coast. The land discovered was named Virginia in honor of Elizabeth, the "virgin queen," though neither ship reached what is now the state of Virginia. Actually, they had sailed to the Albemarle Sound area of North Carolina, near **Roanoke Island** (*see*). The ships reported back that the land was ideal for settlement. However, Raleigh's two attempts to plant a colony on Roanoke Island failed. The first group of colonists deserted, the second group disappeared. He subsequently turned over his proprietary rights to some merchants in 1589. Political enemies in England subsequently convinced **James I** (*see*) that Raleigh was opposed to his succes-

Sir Walter Raleigh

sion to the throne in 1603. As a result, Raleigh was convicted of treason and imprisoned. He was released in 1616 to make another expedition to South America, but his men disobeyed royal orders not to attack any Spanish settlements. On his return, Raleigh was again imprisoned. He was beheaded on October 29, 1618.

REPARTIMIENTO. This was the name given to the Spanish system of land distribution in the New World. With the land, according to royal decree, went all Indians living on it. This resulted in the brutal enslavement of the natives. Queen Isabella (*see* **Ferdinand**) tried to replace the system in 1503 with a policy of *encomienda* (from a Spanish word meaning "to entrust"). In theory, the new policy charged the Spanish masters with the responsibility for the well-being and the religious conversion of the Indians who worked for them. In practice, the Indians suffered even more. Despite a ruling in 1537 by Pope Paul III (1468–1549) that the Indians were "truly men" and should not be enslaved, the Spaniards continued to exploit the labor of the Indians. **Charles I** (*see*) of Spain attempted unsuccessfully in 1542 to revoke the *encomienda* and free the Indians, but the threat of a rebellion by the colonists caused him to retract his edict. When *repartimiento* was again legalized eight years later, all pretense of humanitarianism was dropped, and the starving Indians died by the thousands. "It was hardly possible to walk except over dead men or bones," wrote a priest who had seen the conditions at the mines in Mexico, "and so great were the numbers of the birds and the buzzards that came to eat the bodies of the dead that they cast a huge shadow over the sun."

RIBAUT, Jean (1520?–1565). Ribaut, a French naval captain, was selected to establish a French colony on the coast of Florida. He sailed for the New World in 1562 with three ships and 150 settlers. Ribaut landed north of his intended destination and founded the settlement of Charlesfort, near

Ribaut's ships, in this engraving, are anchored off Port Royal in 1562.

present-day Port Royal, South Carolina. Ribaut returned to France the same year to seek aid for the new colony. However, civil war between the Protestant Huguenots and the Catholics had broken out during his absence. As a result, he was unable to sail again to Charlesfort. When his home town of Dieppe was captured in the autumn of 1562, Ribaut fled to England, where **Elizabeth I** (*see*) encouraged him to join an English expedition headed for the Carolinas. Ribaut refused and was imprisoned in the Tower of London for several years.

Meanwhile, the discouraged settlers in Charlesfort abandoned the colony and sailed for home. A second French expedition later established a new settlement, Fort Caroline, south of the abandoned site. Ribaut set sail for it with a fleet of seven ships after being freed by the British in 1565. His departure alarmed the Spanish, who had colonies nearby in Florida. Led by Pedro Menendez de Aviles (1519–1574), a Spanish fleet attacked Fort Caroline but was repulsed by Ribaut's forces. Ribaut then launched a naval counterattack, leaving the fort un-

guarded. Menendez easily captured the colony by attacking overland. He slaughtered most of the inhabitants. Ribaut, whose ship had been driven ashore off the Florida coast by a violent storm, was subsequently captured and stabbed to death on Menendez's orders.

RICHELIEU, Armand Jean du Plessis de, Cardinal (1585–1642). Richelieu, a cardinal who was able to dominate the French king, played a key role in organizing the Hundred Associates in 1627. This organization was supposed to transport settlers to Canada. The plan failed. The Roman Catholic peasants—who were allowed to emigrate—refused to leave their homes in France. The Protestant Huguenots—who, like the Puritans, were persecuted by the government—were prohibited for political reasons from leaving France. Hence, the early French activities in Canada were largely limited to fur trading. An arrogant and proud man, Richelieu served as France's chief minister (1624–1642) during the reign of Louis XIII (1601–1643). The cardinal's direction of both the nation's foreign and domestic policies resulted in a concentration of the royal power and paved the way for the long, glorious rule of the Sun King, Louis XIV (1638–1715).

ROANOKE ISLAND. Sir Walter Raleigh (*see*) selected this island off the northeastern coast of North Carolina as the site of the first English colony in America. A "citie of Raleigh" was founded in 1585 on the island by a group of colonists who were more interested in finding gold than in establishing a permanent settlement. Their relations with the Indians on the mainland quickly deteriorated, and the group returned to England after 10 months. In 1587, Raleigh dispatched a second expedition under Governor John White. He and about 115 persons moved into the houses and fort that had been built and abandoned by the first group. A month later White returned to England for supplies. Because of England's hostilities with Spain, he did not get back to Roanoke for four years. When he did, there was no trace of the settlers. The only clues were the letters CRO carved on a tree and the word CROATOAN (a nearby island populated by friendly Indians) chiseled on a doorpost. Numerous theories have been advanced as to the fate of the "lost colony," including the possibility that the settlement was destroyed by a Spanish war party. The mystery has never been solved.

ROLFE, John (1585–1622). A farmer of the English colony at Jamestown, Virginia, Rolfe in 1613 discovered a way of curing **tobacco** (*see*) that had vast economic implications. He was soon growing and curing more tobacco than he needed, so he sent a shipment of it to England in 1614. Tobacco soon became the colony's major export. About this time, Rolfe became infatuated with **Pocahontas**, the daughter of the Indian chief **Powhatan** (*see both*). He married her in 1614, explaining that their marriage was "for the good of this plantation, for the honour of our countrie, for the glory of God, for my owne salvation, and for the converting to the true knowledge of God and Jesus Christ, an unbeleeving creature, namely Pokahuntas." When he presented his bride at the court of **James I** (*see*) in London in 1616, Rolfe, a commoner, was reprimanded for marrying royalty without the king's permission. How-

ever, James I relented and accepted the alliance. The marriage cemented a bond with the local Indians and gave the colonists eight years of relative peace. After Pocahontas' death in 1617, Rolfe returned to Virginia. He later remarried and is believed to have been killed in an Indian massacre in 1622. His son by Pocahontas lived to become the ancestor of a long line of Virginia families.

SANDYS, Sir Edwin (1561–1629). A member of the House of Commons under **James I** (*see*) and Charles I (1600–1649), Sandys was instrumental in assisting the early English settlers to immigrate to the New World. He organized the government of Virginia and helped to obtain the charter for the *Mayflower* (*see*). He was later suspected of hostility to the crown, accused of trying to set up a Puritan republic in America, and imprisoned in 1621. His repeated vows of obedience to the king eventually earned him a royal pardon. His younger brother George (1578–1644), a resident of the Virginia colony for a decade, was the first English poet known to have written in America.

SEPARATISTS. These Protestant dissenters, who founded the Plymouth Colony in Massachusetts in 1620, decided to "separate" from the **Church of England** (*see*) because they believed it was still too similar to the Roman Catholic Church in ritual and organization. In this respect, they differed from the **Puritans** (*see*), who wanted to stay within the Anglican Church and "purify" it. Both groups were severely persecuted by **James I** (*see*) and

Charles I (1600–1649). The Separatists, who were concentrated around Gainsborough and Scrooby, fled to Holland. Despite their efforts to escape English tyranny, their leaders were harassed and threatened with imprisonment. In desperation, the Separatists contracted with a London-based company called the Merchant Adventurers to relocate in the New World. Forty-six of them returned to England in 1620 aboard the *Speedwell*. At Southampton, the *Speedwell* was joined by the *Mayflower* (*see*), which was already loaded with emigrants. Many of these people were poor tradesmen and shopowners who sought better conditions in the New World. The Separatists, who called themselves the Saints, referred to the newcomers as the Strangers. The best-known Strangers are John Alden (1599?–1687) and Captain Miles Standish (1584?–1656). After much debate with the sponsoring Merchant Adventurers, the ships finally sailed on August 5. When the *Speedwell* developed leaks, both ships returned to Plymouth, England. The *Speedwell* was left behind, and the Separatists crowded aboard the *Mayflower*. The first landfall in the New World was made on November 21, according to the **Gregorian calendar** (*see*). The settlers, using the Julian calendar, recorded the date as November 11. A month later, on December 21, the **Pilgrims** (*see*), as the *Mayflower*'s 102 passengers would later be known, landed on the Massachusetts coast.

SEVEN CITIES OF CIBOLA. *See* **Cibola**.

SMITH, John (1580–1631). Without John Smith's resourceful leadership and his tact in dealing with the local Indians, the English

As Smith later told the story, Pocahontas saved him from being killed.

colony at **Jamestown** (*see*) would have perished. Smith began his career as a soldier of fortune in Europe. After his return to England in 1603, he helped to form the **Virginia Company of London** (*see*). He sailed in 1606 with the first group of Jamestown settlers. The following year, the captain became a member of the governing council, whose leaders spent more time quarreling among themselves than overseeing the colony. In September, 1607, Smith was a defendant in the first jury trial held in an English colony here. He won the case and was awarded a large sum of money in damages for slander. After learning the local Indian dialects, the captain went foraging to procure food in 1608 and was captured by the Indians. **Pocahontas** (*see*) interceded with her father, **Powhatan** (*see*), and saved Smith's life, although it is possible that what Smith viewed as an attempt to execute him was actually a ceremony making him an honorary tribal chief. Back at Jamestown, a rival faction had Smith arrested again. This time he was charged and convicted of negligence in connection with the deaths of two

men killed by the Indians. On the eve of his hanging, he was reprieved. Smith became president of the ruling council (1608–1609). In this capacity he wrote his *True relation of . . . occurrences in Virginia*, the earliest account of life at Jamestown. He also explored Chesapeake Bay and the Potomac and Rappahannock Rivers. After being injured by exploding gunpowder in 1609, Smith returned to England. The rest of his life was devoted to promoting the colonization of New England. He made two voyages to the region, in 1614 and 1615. His *Description of New England,* written in 1616, called the area the "Countrie of Massachusetts, which is the Paradise of all those parts." The Pilgrims (*see* **Separatists**) later depended on this tract and Smith's other books and maps when they sailed to the New World in 1620. Smith's offer to accompany the Pilgrims was refused because they felt that the presence of the flamboyant adventurer was morally undesirable.

SPANISH ARMADA. This fleet of 130 ships was sent in 1588 by Philip II of Spain (1527–1598) to

pick up troops in the Spanish Netherlands for the invasion of England. Commanded by the Duke of Medina Sidonia (1550–1615), the so-called Invincible Armada sailed into the English Channel in July and was promptly attacked by English ships under the command of such famous English captains as **Hawkins, Drake,** and **Frobisher** (*see all*). The Spanish ships were scattered and thus prevented from reaching Flanders, where the army of invasion was waiting. Eventually, most of the Spanish ships escaped to the north, but the return voyage around Scotland and Ireland was a disaster. Storms scattered the ships and drove many of them onto hostile beaches, where their crews were killed. Many more Spaniards died when their food and water supplies were exhausted. Only half the Armada returned to Spain. The defeat was the end of Spain as a world power.

STUYVESANT, Petrus (1592–1672). Known as Peter to the British, Stuyvesant was an ex-soldier who became the director general of New Netherland, which included all the Dutch holdings in the New World. Stuyvesant's lengthy career in the service of the **Dutch West India Company** (*see*) began in 1635 with a post in Brazil. While he was governor of the Leeward Island of Curaçao, Stuyvesant led an attack on the French-held island of Saint Martin in 1644. During the engagement, he was wounded in the right leg, which had to be amputated. Stuyvesant returned to Holland, where he was fitted with an artificial leg. He was commissioned director general of New Netherland in 1646. Upon his arrival the next year in **New Amsterdam** (*see*), Stuyvesant was cheered by the townspeople,

Petrus Stuyvesant

many of whom rebelled five years later because of his rigid policies. He became involved in a dispute over the settlers' demands for participation in colonial matters. Eventually, he gave in to these demands and established a "burgher government" in 1653. After surrendering to the British in 1664, Stuyvesant returned to Holland to account for his actions as director of the Dutch colonies. He spent his last years in New York.

T

TEMPLE OF THE SUN. The Peruvian Indians believed that the dynasty of the **Incas** (*see*) was descended from Inti, the Sun God. There were many temples to this god throughout the empire, but the most sacred was in Cuzco, the capital city. This temple was the center of the Inca religion. Part of a compound called the Golden Enclosure, the temple measured 350 paces from corner to corner. It contained altars to other Inca deities and the mummies of past Lord Incas. Its walls were covered

with hundreds of gold plates, and gold and silver were used throughout for decoration. The temple was looted in 1533 by the soldiers of **Pizarro** (*see*). The Spanish turned it into a Dominican monastery.

TENOCHTITLAN. The capital of the Aztec Empire contained all the gold and precious stones that the **Aztecs** (*see*) had taken as tribute from neighboring tribes. The 2,500-acre city was situated on an oval island in Lake Texcoco. It was connected to the mainland by three causeways with bridges that could be removed in case of attack. There were more canals than streets, and most of the food was brought into the city in boats. What the Spanish conquistadors first saw as they approached Tenochtitlán in 1519 was an impressive array of high towers looming

over clusters of flat-roofed white houses. Some experts have estimated that the population of the city was 300,000. (London had only 40,000 inhabitants at that time.) The Spanish commander, **Hernando Cortez** (*see*), wrote to **Charles I** (*see*) that the Indians "live almost as we do in Spain and with quite as much orderliness." Cortez was soon forced to change this opinion. The highest tower in the city was the temple to the Aztec god of war, Huitzilopochtli. Here captive warriors were led up 114 steps to an altar on which they were sacrificed. Such human sacrifices were an important part of the religion of the Aztecs. This religious slaughter shocked and disgusted the Spanish. The Aztecs picked Tenochtitlán for their capital about 1320 because their gods had promised a divine sign—a hawk sitting upon

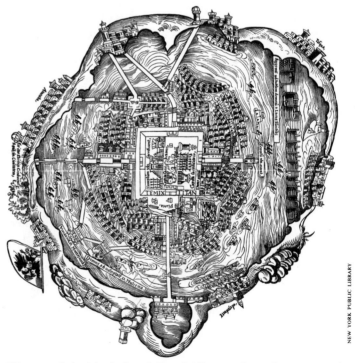

This map of the island city of Tenochtitlán was drawn from memory in 1524, three years after the Spanish invaders had destroyed the Aztec capital.

The European tobacco market enabled the Virginia colonists to survive.

a cactus. The name Tenochtitlán was taken from the Aztec word for "cactus," *tenochtli*. The Spaniards destroyed the city in 1521 and then rebuilt it as their capital for New Spain (Mexico). Today the site of Tenochtitlán is part of Mexico City.

TOBACCO. Well before Columbus discovered the New World, Indians of the Western Hemisphere smoked the dry brown tobacco leaf. The plant was unknown to Europe until Spanish explorers introduced the weed on their return voyages home. The habit of smoking became popular in England about the end of the 16th century, when **Sir Walter Raleigh** (*see*), a fashionable courtier, made it socially acceptable. America's commercial cultivation of tobacco began after **John Rolfe** (*see*) of Virginia perfected a process for curing the South American species *Nicotiana tabacum* in 1613 on his plantation. The plant became a staple export of Virginia and later of both Maryland and North Carolina. Virginia alone soon shipped half a million pounds annually to England. Tobacco played such an important

role in the economic welfare of the colonies that it was often used as legal tender. As one writer observed in 1660, "Tobacco is the current Coyn of Maryland and will sooner purchase Commodities from the Merchant, then money."

TOSCANELLI, Paolo (1397–1482). According to one theory, this noted Florentine geographer received a letter from **Columbus** (*see*) inquiring about a possible sea route to India. Toscanelli wrote to Columbus in 1478, describing how Cathay (China) could be reached by sailing west. Some scholars question the authenticity of Toscanelli's letter.

V

VACA DE CASTRO, Cristobal (?–1558). Disturbed by reports of cruelty and injustice in Peru, **Charles I** (*see*) of Spain in 1540 sent Vaca de Castro, a respected judge, to investigate the regime of **Francisco Pizarro** (*see*). On his arrival there about 1542, Vaca de Castro found that Pizarro had been slain by Spaniards led by Almagro the Lad (1520–1542).

He was the half-caste son of **Diego de Almagro** (*see*), whom Pizarro had executed. Vaca de Castro assumed control of the government, crushed the forces of Almagro the Lad, and executed him in September, 1542. Although a stern, cold man, Vaca de Castro was an able and impartial colonial administrator.

VAN RENSSELAER, Kiliaen (1580?–1644). Van Rensselaer was a member of the **Dutch West India Company** (*see*) who encouraged settlement of the new Dutch colonies in America. He helped establish a patroon system of landholdings in New Netherland in 1629. Under it, tenants could rent land from the patroon, or owner, but were never permitted to own land themselves. Van Rensselaer himself owned vast estates near present-day Albany, New York (*see* **Fort Orange**), but he never visited them. His son Jeremias (1632–1674) was the first Van Rensselaer to live there.

VERRAZANO, Giovanni da (1480?–1527?). The first published description of the northeastern

Giovanni da Verrazano

coast of North America was contained in Verrazano's account of his explorations of the New World. This famous Italian navigator served in the French fleet as a young man. In 1522, he captured two Spanish galleons. The treasure carried aboard them convinced the king of France, Francis I (1494–1547), that America was worth colonizing. He put Verrazano in command of an expedition that set out in 1524 to establish a French empire in the New World. During the voyage, Verrazano discovered the Hudson River and the island of Manhattan, and visited Narragansett Bay. On his return to France, Verrazano wrote an account of the discoveries for the king. It is believed that he was either killed by Indians or hanged as a pirate on a later expedition to the New World.

VESPUCCI, Amerigo (1451–1512). The man after whom the Americas were named (*Amerigo* in Italian means "rich in wheat") made four voyages to the New World and wrote the first popular accounts about it. Employed as a clerk for a commercial company in his hometown of Florence, he came in contact with a number of seagoing adventurers who inspired him to study geography, astronomy, and navigation. He then entered the service of the Spanish king, **Ferdinand** (*see*), and went on an expedition in 1497, on which he claimed, probably erroneously, that he had discovered North America. He next sailed in 1499 with the conquistador **Alonso de Ojeda** (*see*) to Venezuela in search of pearl fisheries. In the employ of Emanuel of Portugal (1469–1521), he took part in an expedition that sailed in 1501 down the coast of Brazil, past the bay of Rio de Janeiro and

Amerigo Vespucci

as far south as Argentina. Vespucci subsequently deduced that a western route to the Orient might lie around the tip of South America, but a fourth voyage to Brazil, in 1503, proved inconclusive. Vespucci's letters describing these explorations were widely circulated in Europe. He included maps and somewhat exaggerated descriptions of the vegetation, animals, and Indian customs. Unlike other explorers, Vespucci believed the places he visited were a new continent and not merely parts of Asia. "These regions," he wrote, "we may rightly call . . . a New World, because our ancestors had no knowledge of them."

VIKINGS. In all probability the Vikings discovered the mainland of North America several hundreds of years before Columbus. Early in the ninth century A.D., these pagan adventurers, who were also known as Norsemen, left Scandinavia to invade Christian Europe. The Vikings were the best mariners in the medieval world, possessing much knowledge about

tides, winds, and celestial navigation. Their warriors, traveling in sailing ships that carried up to 30 oarsmen, dominated Europe for three centuries and crossed the North Atlantic. Because they did not acquire the art of writing on parchment until late in the 11th century, tales of their explorations were passed down by word of mouth. Two principal sagas, based on oral tradition and not written until the 1300s, contain narratives of the western voyages and are mixtures of fact and fiction. The Vikings slowly moved westward by going from island to island. They first reached Iceland, and from there they went to Greenland, where **Eric the Red** (*see*) established the **Greenland Colony** (*see*) in 986. In the same year, according to one saga, a merchant sailor named **Bjarni Herjulfson** (*see*) was driven off course and made a landfall on a new continent. The second saga, which most historians accept, credits **Leif Erikson** (*see*) as the first Viking to arrive, about 1000, at a place where "Day and night were more equally divided than in Greenland or Iceland," and where salmon, "self-sown" wheat, and grapes abounded. The grapes prompted Leif to name the country Vinland the Good. Leif's kinsman, **Thorfinn Karlsefni** (*see*), later attempted to colonize Vinland, but warlike Indians made this impossible. Vinland still has not been identified with certainty. It could have been anywhere from Labrador to Chesapeake Bay. However, recent excavations of artifacts at the northern tip of Newfoundland have provided evidence of the Viking presence in North America and may indicate the site of either Leif's or Karlsefni's camp. After 1030, the Vikings apparently lost interest in America. The Norsemen did not appreciate the importance of their discovery, and the news of it was not circulated in Europe.

The Vinland Map, a discovery announced in 1965 that seemed to confirm early Viking explorations, was declared in 1974 to be a hoax when new chemical tests by Yale University showed that the ink was made sometime after 1920.

VIRGINIA COMPANY OF LONDON. Two cooperating groups of English merchants obtained a charter in 1606 from **James I** (*see*) to colonize British possessions in North America. Their joint corporation was known as the Virginia Company. One branch, the Virginia Company of Plymouth, was to colonize the northern section of the territory but was unsuccessful. The other branch, the Virginia Company of London, known also as the London Company, was responsible for the earliest settlements in Virginia. By selling shares to investors for about $62 in gold each, this company raised enough capital to send abroad the group of colonists that settled in **Jamestown** (*see*) in 1607. The London Company became independent in 1609, and in 1612 it received a revised charter from King James, giving it direct control over the internal affairs of the colony. Jamestown was not successful as a business venture. Most of the settlers were low-paid employees hired for a term of seven years. They could not own land. Some recruits were convicts. As a result, there was little incentive to make Jamestown prosper. The company held lotteries in England to replenish dwindling funds, and it soothed irate investors by publishing pamphlets promising that Virginia was on the verge of prosperity. The company also made a number of reforms. After 1614, the men who chose to stay in the colony were given their own property, and 50 acres of land were offered to shareholders or to emigrants who paid their own passage overseas. In addition, the governor of the colony was instructed to abide by English common law. Although the colony's fortunes improved, King James was still dissatisfied. He dissolved the company in 1624 and made Virginia a crown colony.

WALDSEEMÜLLER, Martin (1470?–1518?). In his *Cosmographiae Introductio* in 1507, this German geographer and map maker published a world map in which he gave the name America to what is now South America. Waldseemüller's reason for thus honoring the Italian explorer **Amerigo Vespucci** (*see*)—rather than **Columbus** (*see*)—was that he probably had access only to Vespucci's travel accounts.

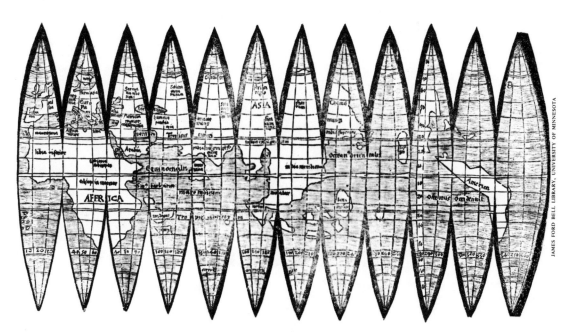

In depicting South America as an island (right) in 1507, Waldseemüller named the New World for an explorer.

NEC IPE·NEC METV